D0806120

BLOOM'S

HOW TO WRITE ABOUT

Sylvia Plath

KIMBERLY CROWLEY

Introduction by Harold Bloom

BLOOM'S
LITERARY CRITICISM
An Infobase Learning Company

Bloom's How to Write about Sylvia Plath

Bloom's Literary Criticism
An imprint of Infobase Learning
132 West 31st Street
New York NY 10001

Library of Congress Cataloging-in-Publication Data

Crowley, Kimberly.
  Bloom's how to write about Sylvia Plath / by Kimberly Crowley ; introduction by Harold Bloom.
        p. cm. — (Bloom's how to write about literature)
  Includes bibliographical references and index.
    ISBN 978-1-60413-767-5 (hardcover : alk. paper) 1. Plath, Sylvia—Criticism and interpretation. 2. Criticism—Authorship. I. Title. II. Title: How to write about Sylvia Plath.
  PS3566.L27Z64 2011
  811'.54—dc23
                            2011027912

Text design by Annie O'Donnell
Cover design by Ben Peterson
Composition by Kerry Casey
Cover printed by Yurchak Printing, Landisville PA
Book printed and bound by Yurchak Printing, Landisville PA
Date printed: December 2011
Printed in the United States of America

10 9 8 7 6 5 4 3 2 1

CONTENTS

SERIES
INTRODUCTION

Bloom's How to Write about Literature series is designed to inspire students to write fine essays on great writers and their works. Each volume in the series begins with an introduction by Harold Bloom, meditating on the challenges and rewards of writing about the volume's subject author. The first chapter then provides detailed instructions on how to write a good essay, including how to find a thesis; how to develop an outline; how to write a good introduction, body text, and conclusions; how to cite sources; and more. The second chapter provides a brief overview of the issues involved in writing about the subject author and then a number of suggestions for paper topics, with accompanying strategies for addressing each topic. Succeeding chapters cover the author's major works.

The paper topics suggested in this book are open ended, and the brief strategies provided are designed to give students a push forward on the writing process rather than a road map to success. The aim of the book is to pose questions, not answer them. Many different kinds of papers could result from each topic. As always, the success of each paper will depend completely on the writer's skill and imagination.

HOW TO WRITE ABOUT SYLVIA PLATH: INTRODUCTION

by Harold Bloom

When I was much younger, I believed firmly that critics should not write about poetry that they did not love, indeed had not loved for a long time. I met and liked Sylvia Plath a third of a century ago in Cambridge, England, and remember then reading her earliest poems with respectful interest. Purchasing *The Colossus* in 1960, I expected a touch more than I received and found the volume too derivative, though accomplished enough. Plath killed herself in 1963, and *Ariel* was published in 1965. I shied away from the book and did not purchase and read it until the early 1970s. Perhaps I would have liked it better then, or could now, if its few merits were not so grossly exaggerated by its many admirers. Perhaps not.

Plath was not Christina Rossetti or even Elizabeth Barrett Browning. If we compare her to an original and powerful poet of her own generation, like the superb May Swenson, then she quite dwindles away. Contemporary reputation is a most inadequate guide to canonical survival. The more fanciful of Plath's admirers have ventured to link her to Emily Dickinson, the most original consciousness and most formidable intellect among all poets in the language since William Blake. A far better comparison would be to Felicia Hemans, English romantic versifier, whose tragic early death gave her a certain glamour for a time. Hemans is remembered today solely for her dramatic lyric, "Casabianca," with its abrupt opening line, "The boy stood on the burning deck," most memorably parodied by the wag who completed the couplet with: "Eating peanuts by the peck." "Lady Lazarus" is the "Casabianca" of my generation and may endure, as such, in some future edition of that marvelous anthology *The Stuffed Owl*.

I do not intend to be contentious, and I have been preceded in my reservations by two critics who are very different both from each other and from myself, Irving Howe and Hugh Kenner. Dr. Samuel Johnson, the sublime of criticism, took on his *Lives of the English Poets* with the understanding that the choice of poets was to be that of the booksellers, whose object was to satisfy the taste of the time. In that spirit, Johnson cheerfully suggested the inclusion of such mighty pens as Yalden and Pomfret to join such eminent hands as Stepney, Sprat, Tickell, Mallet, and Lyttleton. The fashions of each moment in literary history are not unlike each moment in sartorial tradition. Sprat went the way of the bustle. Hysterical intensity, whatever its momentary erotic appeal, is not an affect that endures in verse. Poetry relies on trope and not on sincerity. I have just reread *Ariel*, after some fifteen years, and spontaneously I find myself again murmuring Oscar Wilde's definitive apothegm: "All bad poetry springs from genuine feeling." There are the immensely celebrated pieces, including "Lady Lazarus" with its much-admired conclusion:

> Dying
> Is an art, like everything else.
> I do it exceptionally well.
>
> I do it so it feels like hell.
> I do it so it feels real.
> I guess you could say I've a call.
>
> It's easy enough to do it in a cell.
> It's easy enough to do it and stay put.
> It's the theatrical

Comeback in broad day
To the same place, the same face, the same brute
Amused shout:

"A miracle!"
That knocks me out.
There is a charge

For the eyeing of my scars, there is a charge
For the hearing of my heart—
It really goes.

And there is a charge, a very large charge
For a word or a touch
Or a bit of blood

Or a piece of my hair or my clothes.
So, so, Herr Doktor.
So, Herr Enemy.

I am your opus,
I am your valuable,
The pure gold baby

That melts to a shriek.
I turn and burn.
Do not think I underestimate your great concern.

Ash, ash—
You poke and stir.
Flesh, bone, there is nothing there—

A cake of soap,
A wedding ring,
A gold filling.

Herr God, Herr Lucifer
Beware
Beware.

Out of the ash
I rise with my red hair
And I eat men like air.

Helen Vendler calls this "a tantrum of style" and "a centrifugal spin to further and further reaches of outrage." Those seem to me characteristically kind judgments from a severe student of poetic syntax, the most authoritative in my critical generation. I become lost and doubt my competence to read Plath (or Adrienne Rich and other seers of the school of resentment), when I encounter feminist defenses of Plath's final mode, as here in Mary Lynn Broe:

We lack a critical vocabulary for these rich tones. We lack a critical vocabulary precisely because our society lacks any definition of power which *transforms* rather than *coerces*.

This is to tell me, presumably, that I can write criticism of Emily Dickinson, Elizabeth Bishop, and May Swenson because they manifest a power of coercion, while Plath, Rich, and Alice Walker defeat me because I do not know how to describe and analyze a power of transformation. "Lady Lazarus," with its gratuitous and humanly offensive appropriation of the imagery of Jewish martyrs in Nazi death camps (an appropriation incessant in Plath) seems to me a pure instance of coercive rhetoric, transforming absolutely nothing. That the reader is harangued, not persuaded, is my baffled protest. Barbara Hardy, however, hears an "unfailing grim humor" and a "rationally alert intelligence" in "Lady Lazarus" and its companion poems:

It is present in the great *Ariel* poems: "Lady Lazarus," "Daddy," "Death & Co.," "A Birthday Present," and "The Applicant," which are very outgoing, very deranged, very enlarged. In "Lady Lazarus" the persona is split, and deranged. The split allows the poem to peel off the personal, to impersonate suicidal feeling and generalize it. It is a skill, it is a show, something to look at. The poem seems to be admitting the exhibition-ism of suicide (and death poetry?) as well as the voyeurism of spectators (and readers?). It is also a foul resurrection, stinking of death. This image allows her to horrify us, to complain of being revived, to attack God and confuse him with a doctor, any doctor (bringing round a suicide) and a Doktor in a concentration camp, experimenting in life and death. It moves from Herr Doktor to Herr Enemy and to miracle makers, scien-tists, the torturer who may be a scientist, to Christ, Herr God, and Herr Lucifer (the last two after all collaborated in experiments on Adam, Eve, and Job). They poke and nose around in the ashes, and this is the last indignity, forcing the final threat: "I eat men like air." It is a threat that can intelligibly be made by martyred victims (she has red hair, is Jewish), by phoenixes, by fire, by women. The fusion and dispersal, once more rational and irrational, makes the pattern of controlled derangement, creating not one mirror but a hall of mirrors, all differently distorting, and revealing many horrors.

The poem "Lady Lazarus," here as elsewhere, provokes a mode of criticism that Plath herself deeply contaminates. I have no desire to invoke "The Fallacy of Imitative Form," a legacy of the critic Yvor Win-ters. Plath's fate was poignant; whether "Lady Lazarus" is poignant, or a tantrum, or even a poignant tantrum seems to me an aesthetic question to which a clear answer indeed can be made. If Plath's achievement (and Rich's) is indeed so original and so great that it calls for a new aesthetic, then let that aesthetic come down upon us. Until the aesthetic of resent-ment has achieved itself, the later poetry of Sylvia Plath will abide with its admirers.

HOW TO WRITE A GOOD ESSAY

by Laurie A. Sterling and Kimberly Crowley

While there are many ways to write about literature, most assignments for high school and college English classes call for analytical papers. In these assignments, you are presenting your interpretation of a text to your reader. Your objective is to interpret the text's meaning in order to enhance your reader's understanding and enjoyment of the work. Without exception, strong papers about the meaning of a literary work are built upon a careful, close reading of the text or texts. Careful, analytical reading should always be the first step in your writing process. This volume provides models of such close, analytical reading, and these should help you develop your own skills as a reader and as a writer.

As the examples throughout this book demonstrate, attentive reading entails thinking about and evaluating the formal (textual) aspects of the author's works: theme, character, form, and language. In addition, when writing about a work, many readers choose to move beyond the text itself to consider the work's cultural context. In these instances, writers might explore the historical circumstances of the time period in which the work was written. Alternatively, they might examine the philosophies and ideas that a work addresses. Even in cases where writers explore a work's cultural context, though, papers must still address the more formal aspects of the work itself. A good interpretative essay that evaluates Shakespeare's use of argument in *Cymbeline* cannot simply give a history of the Gallic wars without firmly grounding this discussion in the play

1

itself and using it to show the validity of both Lucius's and the queen's arguments. In other words, any analytical paper about a text, even one that seeks to evaluate the work's cultural context, must also have a firm handle on the work's themes, characters, and language. You must look for and evaluate these aspects of a work, then, as you read a text and as you prepare to write about it.

WRITING ABOUT THEMES

Literary themes are more than just topics or subjects treated in a work; they are attitudes or points about these topics that often structure other elements in a work. Writing about theme therefore requires that you not just identify a topic that a literary work addresses but also discuss what that work says about that topic. For example, if you were writing about the theme of resolutions in *All's Well That Ends Well*, you must not simply discuss the main resolution of the romance between Helena and Bertram but also minor resolutions of issues along the way, such as the king's illness and Parolles's betrayal of his comrades.

When you prepare to write about thematic concerns in a work of literature, you will probably discover that, like most works of literature, your text touches upon other themes in addition to its central theme. These secondary themes also provide rich ground for paper topics. A thematic paper on *All's Well That Ends Well* might consider forgiveness or trickery in the story. While neither of these could be said to be the central theme of the story, they are clearly related to a main theme of nature versus nurture and could provide plenty of good material for papers.

As you prepare to write about themes in literature, you might find a number of strategies helpful. After you identify a theme or themes in the story, you should begin by evaluating how other elements of the story—such as character, point of view, imagery, and symbolism—help develop the theme. You might ask yourself what your own responses are to the author's treatment of the subject matter. Do not neglect the obvious, either: What expectations does the title set up? How does the title help develop thematic concerns? Clearly, the title "A Rose for Emily" says something about the narrator's attitude toward the title character, Emily Grierson, and all she represents.

WRITING ABOUT CHARACTER

Generally, characters are essential components of fiction and drama. (This is not always the case, though; Ray Bradbury's "August 2026: There Will Come Soft Rains" is technically a story without characters, at least any human characters.) Often, you can discuss character in poetry, as in T. S. Eliot's "The Love Song of J. Alfred Prufrock" or Robert Browning's "My Last Duchess." Characters are, however, essential components in Shakespeare's romances. Many writers find that analyzing character is one of the most interesting and engaging ways to work with a piece of literature and to shape a paper. After all, characters generally are human, and we all know something about being human and living in the world. While it is always important to remember that these figures are not real people but creations of the writer's imagination, it can be fruitful to begin evaluating them as you might evaluate a real person. Often you can start with your own response to a character. Did you like or dislike the character? Did you sympathize with the character? Why or why not?

Keep in mind, though, that emotional responses like these are just starting places. To truly explore and evaluate literary characters, you need to return to the formal aspects of the text and evaluate how the author has drawn these characters. The 20th-century writer E. M. Forster coined the terms *flat* characters and *round* characters. Flat characters are static, one-dimensional characters who frequently represent a particular concept or idea. In contrast, round characters are fully drawn and much more realistic characters who frequently change and develop over the course of a work. Are the characters you are studying flat or round? What elements of the characters lead you to this conclusion? Why might the author have drawn characters like this? How does their development affect the meaning of the work? Similarly, you should explore the techniques the author uses to develop characters. Do we hear a character's own words, or do we hear only other characters' assessments of him or her? Or, does the author use an omniscient or limited omniscient narrator to allow us access to the workings of the characters' minds? If so, how does that help develop the characterization? Often you can even evaluate the narrator as a character. How trustworthy are the opinions and assessments of the narrator? You should also think about characters' names. Do they mean anything? If you encounter a hero named Sophia or Sophie, you should probably think about her wisdom (or lack thereof), since *sophia* means "wisdom" in Greek. Similarly, since the name *Sylvia* is derived from the word *sylvan*, meaning "of the wood," you might want to evaluate that character's relationship with nature. Once again, you might look to the title of the work. Does Herman Melville's "Bartleby, the Scrivener" signal anything about Bartleby himself? Is Bartleby adequately defined by his job as scrivener? Is this part of Melville's point? Pursuing questions like these can help you develop thorough papers about characters from psychological, sociological, or more formalistic perspectives.

WRITING ABOUT FORM AND GENRE

Genre, a word derived from French, means "type" or "class." Literary genres are distinctive classes or categories of literary composition. On the most general level, literary works can be divided into the genres of drama, poetry, fiction, and essays, yet in those genres there are classifications that are also referred to as genres. Tragedy and comedy, for example, are genres of drama. Epic, lyric, and pastoral are genres of poetry. *Form*, on the other hand, generally refers to the shape or structure of a work. There are many clearly defined forms of poetry that follow specific patterns of meter, rhyme, and stanza. Sonnets, for example, are poems that follow a fixed form of 14 lines. Sonnets generally follow one of two basic sonnet forms, each with its own distinct rhyme scheme. Haiku is another example of poetic form, traditionally consisting of three unrhymed lines of five, seven, and five syllables.

While you might think that writing about form or genre might leave little room for argument, many of these forms and genres are very fluid. Remember that literature is evolving and ever changing, and so are its forms. As you study poetry, you may find that poets, especially more modern poets, play with traditional poetic forms, bringing about new effects. Similarly, dramatic tragedy was once quite narrowly defined, but over the centuries playwrights have broadened and challenged traditional definitions, changing the shape of tragedy. When Arthur Miller wrote *Death of a Salesman*, many critics challenged the idea that tragic drama could encompass a common man like Willy Loman.

Evaluating how a work of literature fits into or challenges the boundaries of its form or genre can provide you with fruitful avenues of investigation. You might find it helpful to ask why the work does or does not fit into traditional categories. Why might Miller have thought it fitting to write a tragedy of the common man? Similarly, you might compare the content or theme of a work with its form. How well do they work together? Many of Emily Dickinson's poems, for instance, follow the meter of traditional hymns. While some of her poems seem to express traditional religious doctrines, many seem to challenge or strain against traditional conceptions of God and theology. What is the effect, then, of her use of traditional hymn meter?

WRITING ABOUT LANGUAGE, SYMBOLS, AND IMAGERY

No matter what the genre, writers use words as their most basic tool. Language is the most fundamental building block of literature. It is essential that you pay careful attention to the author's language and word choice as you read, reread, and analyze a text. Imagery is language that appeals to the senses. Most commonly, imagery appeals to our sense of vision, creating a mental picture, but authors also use language that appeals to our other senses. Images can be literal or figurative. Literal images use sensory language to describe an actual thing. In the broadest terms, figurative language uses one thing to speak about something else. For example, if I call my boss a snake, I am not saying that he is literally a reptile. Instead, I am using figurative language to communicate my opinions about him. Since we think of snakes as sneaky, slimy, and sinister, I am using the concrete image of a snake to communicate these abstract opinions and impressions.

The two most common figures of speech are similes and metaphors. Both are comparisons between two apparently dissimilar things. Similes are explicit comparisons using the words *like* or *as;* metaphors are implicit comparisons. To return to the previous example, if I say, "My boss, Bob, was waiting for me when I showed up to work five minutes late today—the snake!" I have constructed a metaphor. Writing about his experiences fighting in World War I, Wilfred Owen begins his poem "Dulce et decorum est" with a string of similes: "Bent double, like old beggars under sacks, / Knock-kneed, coughing like hags, we cursed through sludge." Owen's goal was to undercut clichéd notions that war and dying in battle were glorious. Certainly, comparing soldiers to coughing hags and to beggars underscores his point.

"Fog," a short poem by Carl Sandburg, provides a clear example of a metaphor. Sandburg's poem reads:

> The fog comes
> on little cat feet.
>
> It sits looking
> over harbor and city
> on silent haunches
> and then moves on.

Notice how effectively Sandburg conveys surprising impressions of the fog by comparing two seemingly disparate things—the fog and a cat.

Symbols, by contrast, are things that stand for, or represent, other things. Often they represent something intangible, such as concepts or ideas. In everyday life we use and understand symbols easily. Babies at christenings and brides at weddings wear white to represent purity. Think, too, of a dollar bill. The paper itself has no value in and of itself. Instead, that paper bill is a symbol of something else, the precious metal in a nation's coffers. Symbols in literature work similarly. Authors use symbols to evoke more than a simple, straightforward, literal meaning. Characters, objects, and places can all function as symbols. Famous literary examples of symbols include Moby Dick, the white whale of Herman Melville's novel, and the scarlet *A* of Nathaniel Hawthorne's *The Scarlet Letter.* As both of these symbols suggest, a literary symbol cannot be adequately defined or explained by any one meaning. Hester Prynne's Puritan community clearly intends her scarlet *A* as a symbol of her adultery, but as the novel progresses, even her own community reads the letter as representing not just *adultery,* but *able, angel,* and a host of other meanings.

Writing about imagery and symbols requires close attention to the author's language. To prepare a paper on symbolism or imagery in a work, identify and trace the images and symbols and then try to draw some conclusions about how they function. Ask yourself how any symbols or images help contribute to the themes or meanings of the work. What connotations do they carry? How do they affect your reception of the work? Do they shed light on characters or settings? A strong paper on imagery or symbolism will thoroughly consider the use of figures in the text and will try to reach some conclusions about how or why the author uses them.

WRITING ABOUT HISTORY AND CONTEXT

As previously noted, it is possible to write an analytical paper that also considers the work's context. After all, the text was not created in a vacuum. The author lived and wrote in a specific time period and in a specific cultural context and, like all of us, was shaped by that environment. Learning more about the historical and cultural circumstances that surround the author and the work can help illuminate a text and provide you with productive material for a paper. Remember, though, that when you write analytical papers, you should use the context to illuminate the text. Do not lose sight of your goal—to interpret the meaning of the literary work. Use historical or philosophical research as a tool to develop your textual evaluation.

Thoughtful readers often consider how history and culture affected the author's choice and treatment of his or her subject matter. Investigations into the history and context of a work could examine the work's relation to specific historical events, such as the Salem witch trials in seventeenth-century Massachusetts or the restoration of Charles to the British throne in 1660. Bear in mind that historical context is not limited to politics and world events. While knowing about the Vietnam War is certainly helpful in interpreting much of Tim O'Brien's fiction, and some knowledge of the French Revolution clearly illuminates the dynamics of Charles Dickens's *A Tale of Two Cities,* historical context also entails the fabric of daily life. Examining a text in light of gender roles, race relations, class boundaries, or working conditions can give rise to thoughtful and compelling papers. Exploring the conditions of the working class in nineteenth-century England, for example, can provide a particularly effective avenue for writing about Dickens's *Hard Times.*

You can begin thinking about these issues by asking broad questions at first. What do you know about the time period and about the author? What does the editorial apparatus in your text tell you? These might be starting places. Similarly, when specific historical events or dynamics are particularly important to understanding a work but might be somewhat obscure to modern readers, textbooks usually provide notes to explain historical background. These are a good place to start. With this information, ask yourself how these historical facts and circumstances might have affected the author, the presentation of theme, and the presentation of character. How does knowing more about the work's specific historical context illuminate the work? To take a well-known example, understanding the complex attitudes toward slavery during the time Mark Twain wrote *Adventures of Huckleberry Finn* should help you begin to examine issues of race in the text. Additionally, you might compare these attitudes to those of the time in which the novel was set. How might this comparison affect your interpretation of a work written after the abolition of slavery but set before the Civil War?

WRITING ABOUT PHILOSOPHY AND IDEAS

Philosophical concerns are closely related to both historical context and thematic issues. Like historical investigation, philosophical research can provide a useful tool as you analyze a text. For example, an investigation into the working class in Dickens's England might lead you to a topic on the philosophical doctrine of utilitarianism in *Hard Times.* Many other works explore philosophies and ideas quite explicitly. Mary Shelley's famous novel *Frankenstein,* for example, explores John Locke's tabula rasa theory of human knowledge as she portrays the intellectual and emotional development of Victor Frankenstein's creature. As this example indicates, philosophical issues are somewhat more abstract than investigations of theme or historical context. Some other examples of philosophical issues include human free will, the formation of human identity, the nature of sin, or questions of ethics.

Writing about philosophy and ideas might require some outside research, but usually the notes or other material in your text will provide you with basic information, and often footnotes and bibliographies suggest places you can go to read further about the subject. If you have identified a philosophical theme that runs through a text, you might ask yourself how the author develops this theme. Look at character development and the interactions of characters, for example. Similarly, you might examine whether the narrative voice in a work of fiction addresses the philosophical concerns of the text.

WRITING COMPARISON AND CONTRAST ESSAYS

Finally, you might find that comparing and contrasting the works or techniques of an author provides a useful tool for literary analysis. A comparison and contrast essay might compare two characters or themes in a single work, or it might compare the author's treatment of a theme in two works. It might also contrast methods of character development or analyze an author's differing treatment of a philosophical concern in two works. Writing comparison and contrast essays, though, requires some special consideration. While they generally provide you with plenty of material to use, they also come with a built-in trap: the laundry list. These papers often become mere lists of connections between the works. As this chapter will discuss, a strong thesis must make an assertion that you want to prove or validate. A strong comparison/contrast thesis, then, needs to comment on the significance of the similarities and differences you observe. It is not enough merely to assert that the works contain similarities and differences. You might, for example, assert why the similarities and differences are important and explain how they illuminate the works' treatment of theme. Remember, too, that a thesis should not be a statement of the obvious. A comparison/contrast paper that focuses only on very obvious similarities or differences does little to illuminate the connections between the works. Often, an effective method of shaping a strong thesis and argument is to begin your paper by noting the similarities between the works but then to develop a thesis that asserts how these apparently similar elements are different. If, for example, you observe that Emily Dickinson wrote a number of poems about spiders, you might analyze how she uses spider imagery differently in two poems. Similarly, many scholars have noted that Hawthorne created many "mad scientist" characters, men who are so devoted to their science or their art that they lose perspective on all else. A good thesis comparing two of these characters—Aylmer of "The Birth-mark" and Dr. Rappaccini of "Rappaccini's Daughter," for example—might initially identify both characters as examples of Hawthorne's mad scientist type but then argue that their motivations for scientific experimentation differ. If you strive to analyze the similarities or differences, discuss significances, and move beyond the obvious, your paper should move beyond the laundry list trap.

PREPARING TO WRITE

Armed with a clear sense of your task—illuminating the text—and with an understanding of theme, character, language, history, and philosophy, you are ready to approach the writing process. Remember that good writing is grounded in good reading and that close reading takes time, attention, and more than one reading of your text. Read for comprehension first. As you go back and review the work, mark the text to chart the details of the work as well as your reactions. Highlight important passages, repeated words, and image patterns. "Converse" with the text through marginal notes. Mark turns in the plot, ask questions, and make observations about characters, themes, and language. If you are reading from a book that does not belong to you, keep a record of your reactions in a journal or notebook. If you have read a work of literature carefully, paying attention to both the text and the context of the work, you have a leg up on the writing process. Admittedly, at this point, your ideas are probably very broad and undefined, but you have taken an important first step toward writing a strong paper.

Your next step is to focus, to take a broad, perhaps fuzzy, topic and define it more clearly. Even a topic provided by your instructor will need to be focused appropriately. Remember that good writers make the topic their own. There are a number of strategies—often called "invention"—that you can use to develop your own focus. In one such strategy, called *freewriting*, you spend 10 minutes or so just writing about your topic without referring back to the text or your notes. Write whatever comes to mind; the important thing is that you just keep writing. Often this process allows you to develop fresh ideas or approaches to your subject matter. You could also try *brainstorming:* Write down your topic and then list all the related points or ideas you can think of. Include questions, comments, words, important passages or events, and anything else that comes to mind. Let one idea lead to another. In the related technique of *clustering,* or *mapping,* write your topic on a sheet of paper and write related ideas around it. Then list related subpoints under each of these main ideas. Many people then draw arrows to show connections between points. This technique helps you narrow your topic and can also help you organize your ideas. Similarly, asking journalistic questions— Who? What? Where? When? Why? and How?—can develop ideas for topic development.

Thesis Statements

Once you have developed a focused topic, you can begin to think about your thesis statement, the main point or purpose of your paper. It is imperative that you craft a strong thesis, otherwise, your paper will likely be little more than random, disorganized observations about the text. Think of your thesis statement as a kind of road map for your paper. It tells your reader where you are going and how you are going to get there.

To craft a good thesis, you must keep a number of things in mind. First, as the title of this subsection indicates, your paper's thesis should be a statement, an assertion about the text that you want to prove or validate. Beginning writers often formulate a question that they attempt to use as a thesis. For example, a writer considering the recurring mention of the Rosenberg executions for treason in *The Bell Jar* might ask, What is significant about that execution for Esther Greenwood? While thinking about questions like this, it is important to remember that while they can help you pinpoint a thesis statement, they cannot serve as a thesis statement. A question does not adequately explain to your reader what you will be discussing in the paper. When you ask yourself a question in order to formulate a thesis, think about how you would answer the question. For instance, this question might be made into a thesis statement by answering: Since *The Bell Jar* begins with Esther Greenwood's recollection of the story of the execution of the Rosenbergs, Esther obviously sees a connection between their execution and the electroconvulsive therapy she undergoes later in the novel. When Esther equates her treatment with their punishment, she illustrates her belief that she must have done something wrong and that she deserved to be punished for being treasonous in some way, as the Rosenbergs had. This thesis lays out a solid plan for the paper and tells readers about the focus of the discussion. To develop the point made in the thesis, you could include examples from the text that demonstrate Esther's feelings about her therapy and look for ways Plath has connected that therapy to the execution of the Rosenbergs and come up with some ideas about why Plath might have made that comparison.

Second, remember that a good thesis makes an assertion that you need to support. In other words, a good thesis does not state the obvious. If you tried to formulate a thesis about Esther's feelings about her electroconvulsive therapy by stating merely that Esther Greenwood is troubled by the therapy she receives for her depression, you have done nothing but rephrase the obvious. Since the story is clearly centered on the confusion and even resentment Esther feels about her treatment for depression, there would be no point in spending three to five pages supporting that assertion. You might try to develop a thesis from that point by asking yourself some further questions: Why does Esther become troubled enough to attempt suicide? What is it about the treatment she receives for her depression that makes her even more troubled? What changes does Esther undergo after her treatment? Does she believe she has been cured? Such a line of questioning might lead you to a more viable thesis, such as the one in the preceding paragraph.

As the comparison with the road map also suggests, your thesis should appear near the beginning of the paper. In relatively short papers (three to six pages) the thesis almost always appears in the first paragraph. Some writers fall into the trap of saving their thesis for the end, trying to provide a surprise or a big moment of revelation, as if to say, "TA-DA! I've just proved that" in "*The Bell Jar* Esther Greenwood's story illustrates the changing roles of women in the mid-twentieth-century United States by highlighting her confusion and frustration as she tries to decide between pursuing a career or getting married and starting a family." Placing a thesis at the end of an essay can seriously mar the essay's effectiveness. If you fail to define your essay's point and purpose clearly at the beginning, your reader will find it difficult to assess the clarity of your argument and understand the points you are making. When your argument comes as a surprise at the end, you force your reader to reread your essay in order to assess its logic and effectiveness.

Finally, you should avoid using the first person ("I") as you present your thesis. Though it is not strictly wrong to write in the first person, it is difficult to do so gracefully. While writing in the first person, beginning writers often fall into the trap of writing self-reflexive prose (writing *about* their paper *in* their paper). Often this leads to the most dreaded of opening lines: "In this paper I am going to discuss . . ." Not only does this self-reflexive voice make for very awkward prose, it frequently allows writers to boldly announce a topic while completely avoiding a thesis statement. An example might be a paper that begins as follows: In *The Bell Jar*, Sylvia Plath tells the story of Esther Greenwood, a young woman trying to decide what to do with her life—pursue a career as a writer or get married and become a mother. In this paper, I will attempt to explain how Esther's dilemma shows how women's roles were changing at this time. The author of this paper has done little more than announce a general topic for the paper (Esther's confusion about what to do with her life). While the last sentence might be a thesis, the writer fails to present an opinion about the significance of Esther's feelings. To improve this "thesis," the writer would need to back up a couple of steps. The writer should examine the story and draw conclusions about Esther's situation before crafting the thesis. After carefully examining key passages in the story, the writer might determine that Esther feels pressured by the culture in which she lives to give up her personal freedom to pursue marriage and motherhood. This writer would also do well to theorize about what is being said about women's roles in the novel. By looking at how other women, like Mrs. Greenwood and Dodo Conway, behave in the novel, the writer of this paper could find solid grounds for comparing Esther's ideas about being fulfilled to those of other women. The writer might then craft a thesis such as this: Esther Greenwood's struggle to decide what to do with her life in The Bell Jar is a commentary on the changing roles of women in the United States in the 1950s and 1960s. Esther's fears that her personal goals and freedoms would be sacrificed if she got married illustrate how societal expectations for women were upset by new ideas about fulfillment for women.

Outlines

While developing a strong, thoughtful thesis early in your writing process should help focus your paper, outlining provides an essential tool for logically shaping that paper. A good outline helps you see—and develop—the relationships among the points in your argument and assures you that your paper flows logically and coherently. Outlining not only helps place your points in a logical order but also helps you subordinate supporting points, weed out any irrelevant points, and decide if there are any necessary points that are missing from your argument. Most of us are familiar with formal outlines that use numerical and letter designations for each point. However, there are different types of outlines; you may find that an informal outline is a more useful tool for you. What is important, though, is that you spend the time to develop some sort of outline—formal or informal.

Remember that an outline is a tool to help you shape and write a strong paper. If you do not spend sufficient time planning your supporting points and shaping the arrangement of those points, you will most likely construct a vague, unfocused outline that provides little, if any, help with the writing of the paper. Consider the following example.

Thesis: Esther Greenwood's struggle to decide what to do with her life in *The Bell Jar* is a commentary on the changing roles of women in the United States in the 1950s and 1960s. Esther's fears that her personal goals and freedoms would be sacrificed if she got married illustrate how societal expectations for women were upset by new ideas about fulfillment for women.

   I.   Introduction and thesis

  II.   Buddy Willard
      A. Her mother approves of him
      B. He goes to college nearby

 III. Esther's mother
      A. Supports Esther's treatment
      B. Does not understand Esther's writing

 IV. Esther's trip to New York City
      A. She experiences a lot of things that she
         cannot in her home in the suburbs
      B. Gets to forget about her family life
      C. Sex

  V.   Death of Esther's father

 VI. Conclusion

This outline has a number of flaws. First, the major topics labeled with the Roman numerals are not arranged in a logical order. Since the paper is focusing on how Esther's situation is reflective of changing roles of women, the major points of this outline should address that subject more clearly and the supporting points, the A, B, C, etc., should work to clarify and provide examples. In this case, starting with Buddy Willard makes no sense; starting with Esther's trip to New York would be more logical because it is the starting point for Esther's story. Points A, B, and C under Roman numeral 4 do not really address the best points to use from Esther's trip to New York; these do not really emphasize how that trip affected her ideas about her future. Discussing Buddy Willard in this essay is a good idea, but including him as Roman numeral 2 misrepresents his role in this essay. And while a discussion of Esther's mother is a good thing to include, the supporting points offered here do not fit with the focus of the paper. Finally, there should be a section that discusses what Esther sees as the traditional roles for women. A discussion of Esther's father's death could also be significant in this essay, but without any supporting points it is not clear *how*. None of the sections provides much information about the content of the argument, and it seems likely that the writer has not given sufficient thought to the content of the paper.

A better start to this outline might be the following:

Thesis: Esther Greenwood's struggle to decide what to do with her life in *The Bell Jar* is a commentary on the changing roles of women in the United States in the 1950s and 1960s. Esther's fears that her personal goals and freedoms would be sacrificed if she got married illustrate how societal expectations for women were upset by new ideas about fulfillment for women.

    I.   Introduction and thesis

   II.   Esther's trip to New York City
        A. Earns the trip because of her abilities
           as a writer

    B. Works for a women's magazine

    C. Jay Cee as a role model for Esther

    D. The other girls there represent different roles for women

III. Esther's mother

    A. Seems happy when Esther is not accepted to the summer writing program

    B. Teaches secretarial skills, so she has a job but in it she teaches typical work for women

    C. Dodo Conway as another mother figure who typifies women's roles

IV. Esther's apprehension about marriage

    A. Buddy Willard's comment about not wanting her to write when she's a wife and mother

    B. Double standard—Buddy's affair with the waitress

    C. Cannot stand the thought of a summer in the suburbs

V. Death of Esther's father

    A. An example of betrayal by a man

    B. No role model of a husband and father for her to use as a guide

VI. Conclusion

This new outline would prove much more helpful when it came time to write the paper.

An outline like this could be shaped into an even more useful tool if the writer fleshed out the argument by providing specific examples from the text to support each point. Once you have listed your main point and your supporting ideas, develop this raw material by listing related supporting ideas and material under each of those main headings.

From there, arrange the material in subsections and order the material logically.

For example, you might begin with one of the theses cited above: *In The Bell Jar,* Esther Greenwood begins the story of her experiences by referring to the execution of the Rosenbergs by electrocution. By doing so, Esther equates her electroconvulsive treatment with their punishment, suggesting she believes she, like the Rosenbergs, is being punished for treason in some way. As noted above, this thesis supplies a framework for how the discussion could be best organized: You could start by pointing out Esther's reaction to the idea of electrocution and follow that up with examples of how Esther sees her therapy as punishment. You might begin your outline, then, with topic headings such as these: (1) connections to Rosenberg execution, (2) Esther's "treason" by refusing to conform, (3) Plath's incorporation of cold war politics into the novel, (4) Esther's life after the treatment. Under each of those headings you could list ideas that support the particular point. Be sure to include references to parts of the text that help build your case.

An informal outline might look like this:

Thesis: In *The Bell Jar,* Esther Greenwood begins the story of her experiences by referring to the execution of the Rosenbergs by electrocution. By doing so, Esther equates her electroconvulsive treatment with their punishment, suggesting she believes she, like the Rosenbergs, is being punished for treason in some way.

Introduction and thesis

1. Esther's horror at the Rosenberg execution
   - Electrocution as unimaginable ("being burned alive")
   - The story is being told by Esther from the present, so this is her recollection of events, meaning she has already experienced

the ECT when she is recalling her horror at
the execution
- Not quite sure exactly what it was the
  Rosenbergs did to deserve the punishment
- She knew there was something wrong because
  she kept thinking about the Rosenbergs
  that summer

2. Esther's "treason" by refusing to conform
   - Her suicide attempt
     ○ Hiding herself away in the house, she
       creates an alias (Elly Higginbottom)
       while she is in New York so the men
       she meets there do not really know
       her
   - She does not really want to marry Buddy
     Willard, even though he is perfect husband
     material
     ○ Buddy's comments about losing her
       desire to write poetry after she's
       married and becomes a mother—she
       thinks of it as brainwashing
   - She cannot stand the thought of spending
     the summer in the suburbs
     ○ When she is at home she watches Dodo
       Conway, the ultimate mother figure
     ○ Esther's thoughts that children made
       her sick
     ○ Her thoughts of strangling her mother
       in her sleep to end the oppressive
       presence in her life

3. Plath's incorporation of the cold war politics
   into the novel
   - The relationship between Esther and her
     mother becomes a version of the cold war
   - Views of marriage as a "totalitarian state"
   - Esther sees her mother as the enemy

- Her mother's lack of concern when Esther is not accepted into the writing program, which could have been Esther's chance to become a poet
- Mrs. Greenwood is the first person she is aware of when she is pulled out from the hiding spot she has chosen when she attempts suicide, so in a way her mother has foiled her escape attempt and drags her back to the life she wanted to end

4. Esther's life after the treatment—has she been cured?
   - Narrates the story as a recollection or a retelling of a story from her past
   - Talks about the baby and the house, so she is presumably a wife and mother now, even though she resisted it earlier
   - When she leaves the asylum, her cure is not assured because all is question marks
     - Still some ambiguity about her fate since she does not talk much about her present, other than vague references to when she was sick
   - Part of her was, actually, executed if she ended up in that "totalitarian state" she took to be marriage when she was talking with Buddy Willard

Conclusion:
   - Esther's horror at the execution of the Rosenbergs mirrors the horror she feels at her own electrocution, leaving her to feel she is being punished, not treated
   - Esther was at war with the lifestyle her mother embodied, which meant to Esther a

lack of freedom and liberty (living in that "totalitarian state")

- In the end, authority won out because Esther is presumably a wife and mother, not a poet. She looks back at her stint at being a writer (the trip to New York City) resulting in silly gifts
- Her "Alien nature" (Macpherson) has presumably been controlled by electrocution, but there is no definite word on Esther's state of mind, so her fate is still not clearly defined

You would set about writing a formal outline with a similar process, though in the final stages you would label the headings differently. A formal outline for a paper that argues the thesis about *The Bell Jar* cited above—that Esther sees her treatment as punishment for treason against societal expectations for her—might look like this:

Thesis: Esther Greenwood's struggle to decide what to do with her life in *The Bell Jar* is a commentary on the changing roles of women in the United States in the 1950s and 1960s. Esther's fears that her personal goals and freedoms would be sacrificed if she got married illustrate how societal expectations for women were upset by new ideas about fulfillment for women.

   I. Introduction and thesis

  II. Esther's trip to New York City as an opportunity for her to see what options were available outside her suburban home
      A. Esther as a professional or in a traditional role
         1. She won the trip because of her ability as a writer

    2. Many of the other girls there see this as a chance to find love and marriage in the big city

  B. Working for a woman's magazine

    1. Esther's sampling life as a professional woman

    2. Still dependent on traditional roles of women, since her audience is largely housewives

  C. Jay Cee, the symbol of the new career woman

    1. Role model and mentor for Esther

    2. Although powerful, still constrained by her role as wife

    3. Supportive of Esther, yet Esther is still disappointed by her adherence to traditional roles at times

  D. The other girls there represent different roles for women

    1. Doreen, who breaks the rules and plays the vamp (very liberated)

    2. Betsy, the pure Kansas girl who follows the rules (very controlled)

    3. Esther's loyalties switch back and forth between the two girls during her trip; to herself she pledges allegiance to each girl several times

III. Esther's mother as symbolic of everything Esther does not want to be, and also the main authority figure in Esther's life, so she has a lot of control over Esther

  A. Tells Esther she has not made it into the summer writing program immediately upon her arrival home

1. Esther seems to think her mother enjoys this
   B. Earns a living to support her family, yet she is not a professional woman
      1. Teaches secretarial skills
      2. Reinforces traditional roles for women
      3. Agrees to the treatment for Esther to try to make her more normal (meaning she would want what every other normal girl wants)
   C. Dodo Conway as everything Esther does not want to be
      1. Mother of seven children
      2. Lives in the suburbs in a house that is too big, with a family that is too big, driving a car that looks like a hearse (it is that car that brings Esther home from the asylum)

IV. Esther has no desire to get married and have children
   A. Buddy Willard seems like the perfect potential husband for her
      1. He tells her she will not want to write poetry when she is a wife and mother (judging by the way she is narrating her story, he was correct)
      2. She wonders if women really are brainwashed and end up in a "totalitarian state" when they get married
   B. Esther is aware of double standards for men and for women
      1. She feels betrayed when she finds out about Buddy's affair with the waitress

2. Her anger at Buddy is not because she is jealous but because he has pretended to be pure and chaste yet is allowed not to be

C. Cannot stand the thought of a summer in the suburbs

1. It is after she finds out she will not be going to pursue her writing career at the workshop that she becomes depressed and attempts suicide

2. She is forced to witness the lives of women like her mother and Dodo Conway

V. Death of Esther's father

A. His death felt like abandonment

1. Her mother had never cried and thus Esther had never cried for his death

2. Esther sees it as up to her to mourn since her mother did not

B. No role model of a husband and father for her to use as a guide

1. She thinks of all the things he would have taught her if he had lived (German, Greek, Latin)

VI. Conclusion

As in the previous sample outline, the thesis provided the seeds of a structure, and the writer was careful to arrange the supporting points in a logical manner, showing the relationships among the ideas in the paper.

Body Paragraphs

Once your outline is complete, you can begin drafting your paper. Paragraphs, units of related sentences, are the building blocks of a good paper, and as you draft you should keep in mind both the function and the qualities of good paragraphs. Paragraphs help you chart and control the shape and content of your essay, and they help the reader see your organization and your logic. You should begin a new paragraph whenever you move from one major point to another. In longer, more complex essays you might use a group of related paragraphs to support major points. Remember that in addition to being adequately developed, a good paragraph is both unified and coherent.

Unified Paragraphs

Each paragraph must be centered on one idea or point, and a unified paragraph carefully focuses on and develops this central idea without including extraneous ideas or tangents. For beginning writers, the best way to ensure that you are constructing unified paragraphs is to include a topic sentence in each paragraph. This topic sentence should convey the main point of the paragraph, and every sentence in the paragraph should relate to that topic sentence. Any sentence that strays from the central topic does not belong in the paragraph and needs to be revised or deleted. Consider the following paragraph describing how Esther's treatment seems to her like a punishment, as Julius and Ethel Rosenberg were punished for their treason. Notice how the paragraph veers away from the main point:

> Esther sees her inability to fit in with societal norms,
> especially her resistance to marriage and children,
> as the kind of treason that brings on her punishment
> in the form of electroconvulsive therapy. Her fixation
> on the Rosenbergs makes it likely she wondered about
> their guilt. Pat Macpherson argues that Esther believes
> the Rosenbergs were "scapegoated as spies, Communists,
> traitors in our midst, with their Jewishness and Ethel
> Rosenberg's strong womanhood seen as part of the Alien
> nature of this Enemy Within" (2). When the status quo
> is being threatened, it is important to have examples
> that reinforce the ideals and also demonstrate what
> happens to those who threaten those ideals. When Esther
> is in the asylum, Joan's preoccupation with her suicide

attempt shows her how much of an impact she has had on
Joan. Knowing that changes the way Esther thinks about
her life.

Although the paragraph begins solidly and the first sentence contains its
central idea, the author goes on a tangent in the paragraph's last two sentences. If the paragraph's main point is that Esther sees her inability to fit
in as a crime akin to treason, there is a noticeable spot where that point
is dropped and the writer goes on a tangent. The sentences about Joan
stray from the main point forecasted by the first sentence and should be
deleted from this paragraph.

Coherent Paragraphs

In addition to shaping unified paragraphs, you must also craft coherent
paragraphs that develop their points logically with sentences that flow
smoothly into one another. Coherence depends on the order of your sentences, but it is not the only factor that lends the paragraph coherence.
You also need to craft your prose to help the reader see the relationship
among the sentences.

Consider the following paragraph about Esther's feelings that she is
unable to fit in to the society around her and is thus guilty of something
terrible. Notice how the writer uses the same ideas as the paragraph
above yet fails to help the reader see the relationships among the points:

Esther almost feels like a foreigner because she does
not understand the culture she is living in. She does
not want to marry Buddy—she does not want to marry
anyone—and children make her sick. She thinks about
the Rosenbergs, saying, "It had nothing to do with me,
but I couldn't help wondering what it would be like,
being burned alive along all your nerves" (Plath 1).
The Rosenbergs committed treason and were put to death.
As Linda Wagner-Martin points out, their electrocution
was "an event . . . that foreshadows Esther's own
electroconvulsive shock treatments later that same
summer" (34). Esther makes the connection between the
two events in her own mind, which shows how she feels

```
her therapy is a form of punishment instead of a way of
making her better. She might not even realize exactly
what is wrong with her.
```

This paragraph demonstrates that unity alone does not guarantee paragraph effectiveness. The argument is hard to follow because the author fails both to show connections between the sentences and to indicate how they work to support the overall point.

A number of techniques are available to aid paragraph coherence. Careful use of transitional words and phrases is essential. You can use transitional flags to introduce an example or an illustration (*for example, for instance*), to amplify a point or add another phase of the same idea (*additionally, furthermore, next, similarly, finally, then*), to indicate a conclusion or a result (*therefore, as a result, thus, in other words*), to signal a contrast or a qualification (*on the other hand, nevertheless, despite this, on the contrary, still, however, conversely*), to signal a comparison (*likewise, in comparison, similarly*), and to indicate a movement in time (*afterward, earlier, eventually, finally, later, subsequently, until*).

In addition to transitional flags, careful use of pronouns aids coherence and flow. If you were writing about *The Wizard of Oz*, you would not want to keep repeating the phrase *the witch* or the name *Dorothy*. Careful substitution of the pronoun *she* in these instances can aid coherence. A word of warning, though: When you substitute pronouns for proper names, always be sure that your pronoun reference is clear. In a paragraph that discusses both Dorothy and the witch, substituting *she* could lead to confusion. Make sure that it is clear to whom the pronoun refers. Generally, the pronoun refers to the last proper noun you have used.

While repeating the same name over and over again can lead to awkward, boring prose, it is possible to use repetition to help your paragraph's coherence. Careful repetition of important words or phrases can lend coherence to your paragraph by reminding readers of your key points. Admittedly, it takes some practice to use this technique effectively. You may find that reading your prose aloud can help you develop an ear for the effective use of repetition.

To see how helpful transitional aids are, compare the paragraph below to the preceding one about how Esther compares her electroconvulsive therapy to the execution of the Rosenbergs. Notice how the author works with the same ideas and quotations but shapes them into a much more coherent paragraph whose point is clearer and easier to follow:

Because she feels unable to fulfill both her own desires and those that society, and especially her mother, has deemed appropriate for her, Esther feels almost like a foreigner with inappropriate allegiances. She does not want to marry Buddy—she does not want to marry anyone—and children make her sick. Since that is what she is supposed to want, she feels as if she is committing a form of treason. This becomes clear when she thinks about the execution of the Rosenbergs, saying, "It had nothing to do with me, but I couldn't help wondering what it would be like, being burned alive along all your nerves" (Plath 1). As Linda Wagner-Martin points out, their electrocution was "an event . . . that foreshadows Esther's own electroconvulsive shock treatments later that same summer" (34). It is obvious that Esther feels a connection to the Rosenbergs, reinforcing the idea that she sees the similarity in her own treatment and their electrocution. This connection also demonstrates how she feels her therapy is a form of punishment for her own particular form of treason instead of a way of making her better.

Similarly, the following paragraph from a paper on Dodo Conway's role in *The Bell Jar* demonstrates both unity and coherence. In it, the author argues that Dodo's presence in Esther's life, especially during the summer Esther spends at home, is particularly symbolic because Dodo stands for everything Esther does not want:

Readers are introduced to Dodo Conway when Esther describes her as "a Catholic who had gone to Barnard and then married an architect who had gone to Columbia" (Plath 116). By pointing out the fact that Dodo had gone to a prestigious school and then became a wife and mother of six (with a seventh child on the way), Esther makes a rather obvious comment about Dodo's choices. Rather than a career that would put her education to good use, Dodo has instead chosen what Esther describes as "the whole sprawling paraphernalia of suburban childhood" (Plath 116). Dodo stands for everything Esther is rebelling against as she ponders her ambition to become a professional writer. The fact that it is Dodo who drives Esther and her mother to and from the hospital where Esther receives her electroconvulsive therapy is significant too. Dodo and Mrs. Greenwood, the women Esther least wants to emulate, are the ones who are there to make sure she gets the treatments that will cure her so she can want to become more like them after all.

Introductions

Introductions present particular challenges for writers. Generally, your introduction should do two things: capture your reader's attention and explain the main point of your essay. In other words, while your introduction should contain your thesis, it needs to do a bit more work than that. You are likely to find that starting that first paragraph is one of the most difficult parts of the paper. It is hard to face that blank page or screen, and as a result, many beginning writers, in desperation to start somewhere, start with overly broad, general statements. While it is often a good strategy to start with more general subject matter and narrow your focus, do not begin with broad, sweeping statements such as: Many people struggle with society's expectations for them. Such sentences are nothing but empty filler. They begin to fill the blank page, but they do nothing to advance your argument. Instead, you should try to gain your readers' interest. Some writers like to begin with a pertinent quotation or with a relevant question. Or, you might begin with an introduction of the topic you will discuss. If you are writing about how Plath portrays the relationship between Esther and her mother as a cold war, for instance, you might begin by talking about why Esther feels her mother is against her and how Plath equates those feelings to the cold war going on in the 1950s and 1960s. Another common trap to avoid is depending on your title to introduce the author and the text you are writing about. Always include the work's author and title in your opening paragraph.

Compare the effectiveness of the following introductions.

1) Young people have always thought that the older generation did not understand them and is even out to get them. Daughters and mothers especially seem to have this problem. Young people also have worries about fitting in, which can make those relationships with parents even more tense. In the novel, Esther does not fit in and that causes her problems, especially with her mother. When she refuses to do what is expected of her by society, she feels like she gets punished by having to undergo shock therapy. Since her mother allows it to happen, Esther feels like she is at war with her rather than being helped by her. When Plath starts Esther's story with a headline about the execution of the Rosenbergs, she draws a clear parallel between Esther's treatment and their electrocution.

2) The cold war that gripped the United States in the 1950s and 1960s was a major political issue. In *The Bell Jar,* Plath uses the cold war as a corollary for the relationship between Esther Greenwood and her mother. According to Jacqueline Rose, Plath puts Esther in a specific political position, emphasizing her "revulsion at the execution of those alleged Communist spies," the Rosenbergs (195). Esther's refusal to bow to her mother's expectations makes their relationship a sort of war; like the actual cold war, the battle between the two is one of ideologies. By framing her story with the electrocution of the Rosenbergs for treason, Esther suggests that the electroconvulsive therapy she undergoes is a form of electrocution—punishment

for betraying her mother's ideological stance on
marriage and motherhood. To Esther, her mother's
support of that therapy makes her a party to the
punishment and, in essence, an enemy rather than
an ally.

The first introduction begins with a vague, overly broad sentence; cites unclear, undeveloped examples; and then moves abruptly to the thesis. Notice, too, how a reader deprived of the paper's title does not know the title of the work that the paper will analyze. The second introduction works with the same material and thesis but provides more detail and is consequently much more interesting. It begins by discussing the way Plath incorporates the cold war and the execution of the Rosenbergs into Esther's story. The paragraph ends with the thesis and names both the author and the title of the work to be discussed.

The paragraph below provides another example of an opening strategy. It begins by introducing the author and the text it will analyze, and then it moves on to provide some necessary background information before introducing its thesis.

The theme of treason is a prominent one in Sylvia Plath's
The Bell Jar. The main character and narrator, Esther
Greenwood, opens her story with a flashback of the
news stories about Julius and Ethel Rosenberg, famously
executed for treason against the United States during
the cold war that followed World War II. During the
1950s and 1960s, the cold war was a basically non-violent
battle between communist governments like those of Cuba
and the former Soviet Union and democratic governments
like those of the United States and England. As readers
find out more about Esther, it seems as if she is
caught up in her own cold war. By beginning her story
with the Rosenbergs' execution by electrocution, Esther
illustrates how she feels her own psychiatric treatment
was a form of punishment by electrocution for treason.
In the cold war in Esther's life, her mother, the main
authority figure in her life, becomes the embodiment of

what she is fighting against and thus symbolic of what
she sees as threatening what she believes in, including
her ideas about personal freedom.

As Plath herself says of introductions, their purpose is "to indicate topic of discussion, to give as much information as you can on the limitations of topic; to set, or at least hint, *tone* of following" ("Teaching Notes").

Conclusions

Conclusions present another series of challenges for writers. No doubt you have heard the adage about writing papers: "Tell us what you are going to say, say it, and then tell us what you've said." While this formula does not necessarily result in bad papers, it does not often result in good ones, either. It will almost certainly result in boring papers (especially boring conclusions). If you have done a good job establishing your points in the body of the paper, the reader already knows and understands your argument. There is no need to merely reiterate. Do not just summarize your main points in your conclusion. A boring and mechanical conclusion does nothing to advance your argument or interest your reader. Consider the following conclusion to the paper about Esther's cold war with her mother in *The Bell Jar:*

In conclusion, Plath's *The Bell Jar* tells the story
of a daughter's resentment at her mother allowing her
to undergo electroconvulsive therapy. Because of that,
Esther feels as if she is being punished for being
different and relates that punishment to the Rosenbergs'
famous execution for treason.

Besides starting with a mechanical transitional device, this conclusion does little more than summarize the main points of the outline (and it does not even touch on all of them). It is incomplete and uninteresting.

Instead, your conclusion should add something to your paper. A good tactic is to build upon the points you have been arguing. Asking "why?" often helps you draw further conclusions. You might also speculate on other directions in which to take your topic by tying it into larger issues. You might do this by envisioning your paper as just one section of a longer essay. For example, in the paper on *The Bell Jar* you could explain how Esther's treatment seems to have cured her. You might also point out that even though readers are led to believe that Esther is living a normal life now, she is still troubled by what happened to her. In the following conclusion to the paper on *The Bell Jar* the author discusses how Esther has presumably been cured because she is now living a normal life and how Plath hints that even though she's been "cured" and made suitable for a normal life, Esther has not forgotten about the dreams she had before her treatment:

> Through Esther's experience, Plath shows that the best way one can appear normal and able to take care of herself is by doing what she is told. When Esther abandons her antisocial behavior and becomes more obedient and more like her mother and Dodo Conway, she is deemed normal and thus cured. But Esther has not completely forgotten about her previous life, before her treatment, as demonstrated by her wistful recollection of the trip to New York City in the first pages of the book. By including that quick reference about the gifts she received during her stay in New York, "later, when I was all right again, I brought them out and I still have them around the house" (3), Plath shows that even though Esther has become a version of her mother and Dodo, she still clings to that rebellious self, the version of her self that wanted none of the trappings of suburban, middle-class life.

Similarly, in the following conclusion to a paper examining treason in *The Bell Jar*, the author comments on the ambiguity still present for Esther Greenwood after she undergoes the electroconvulsive therapy meant to cure her:

> By framing her own experiences with the execution of the Rosenbergs, Esther shows her preoccupation with their situation. She does not really protest the executions, but she does immediately show a bit of solidarity with

them as she talks about how awful it would be to be "burned alive" (Plath 1). This ambiguity about the Rosenbergs and their fate shows Esther's ambiguity about her own situation. At the end of the book, she contemplates being released from the treatment center, thinking, "I had hoped, at my departure, I would feel sure and knowledgeable about everything that lay ahead—after all, I had been 'analyzed.' Instead, all I could see were question marks" (Plath 243). In the end, it seems that Esther's mother's side—the side that demanded treatment for Esther to make her more like them—has won. But as much as it appears Esther has been won over, there is still some doubt about where her allegiances truly lie, even in her own mind.

For Plath, it is a conclusion's "job to restate, as adroitly as possible, the principle matter . . . of preceding text" ("Teaching Notes").

Citations and Formatting

Using Primary Sources

As the examples included in this chapter indicate, strong papers on literary texts incorporate quotations from the text in order to support their points. It is not enough for you to assert your interpretation without providing support or evidence from the text. Without well-chosen quotations to support your argument you are, in effect, saying to the reader, "Take my word for it." It is important to use quotations thoughtfully and selectively. Remember that the paper presents *your* argument, so choose quotations that support *your* assertions. Do not let the author's voice overwhelm your own. With that caution in mind, there are some guidelines you should follow to ensure that you use quotations clearly and effectively.

Integrate Quotations

Quotations should always be integrated into your own prose. Do not just drop them into your paper without introduction or comment. Otherwise, it is unlikely that your reader will see their function. You can integrate textual support easily and clearly with identifying tags, short phrases that identify the speaker. For example:

> Esther described Miss Norris's reaction; "She just stared straight ahead of her in a polite way."

While this tag appears before the quotation, you can also use tags after or in the middle of the quoted text, as the following examples demonstrate:

> "I'd rather stand," says Esther.

> "Oh, there you are," says the nurse to Esther. "Visiting Miss Norris. How nice!"

You can also use a colon to formally introduce a quotation:

> Esther seemed to distrust Dr. Nolan's vow to come with her: "Promise you'll be there."

When you quote brief sections of poems (three lines or fewer), use slash marks to indicate the line breaks in the poem:

> As the poem begins, Plath frets at the task ahead of her: "I shall never get you put together entirely, / Pieced, glued, and properly jointed."

Longer quotations (more than four lines of prose or three lines of poetry) should be set off from the rest of your paper in a block quotation. Double-space before you begin the passage, indent it 10 spaces from your left-hand margin, and double-space the passage itself. Because the indentation signals the inclusion of a quotation, do not use quotation marks around the cited passage. Use a colon to introduce the passage:

> Esther attempts to explain her efforts to rearrange the women's flowers:

> I was opening my mouth to explain that I had
> thrown a bunch of dead larkspur in the sink, and
> that some of the vases I had weeded out looked
> skimpy, there were so few flowers left, so I had
> joined a few of the bouquets together to fill them
> out, when the swinging door flew open and a nurse
> stalked in to see what the commotion was.

Rather than being seen as thoughtful, Esther's actions
anger the patients, further demonstrating how what
seems logical or even natural to her is seen by others
as evidence that there is something wrong with her and
the way she thinks.

Plath describes her efforts to get to know and understand
her father by piecing him together:

> Perhaps you consider yourself an oracle,
> Mouthpiece of the dead, or of some god or other.
> Thirty years now I have labored.
> To dredge the silt from your throat.
> I am none the wiser.

Obviously she sees her attempts as unsuccessful.

It is also important to interpret quotations after you introduce them
and explain how they help advance your point. You cannot assume that
your reader will interpret the quotations the same way that you do.

Quote Accurately

Always quote accurately. Anything within quotations marks must be the
author's exact words. There are, however, some rules to follow if you need
to modify the quotation to fit into your prose.

1. Use brackets to indicate any material that might have been
   added to the author's exact wording. For example, if you need

to add any words to the quotation or alter it grammatically to allow it to fit into your prose, indicate your changes in brackets:

> Esther considers the trustworthiness of the man giving her skiing lessons: "Then I remembered that at medical school Buddy [her boyfriend] had won a prize for persuading the most relatives of dead people to have their dead ones cut up whether they needed it or not, in the interest of science."

2. Conversely, if you choose to omit any words from the quotation, use ellipses (three spaced periods) to indicate missing words or phrases:

> As she is wheeled to the room where she will receive her treatment, Esther "tried to ask him what the shock treatment would be like, but . . . no words came out."

3. If you delete a sentence or more, use the ellipses after a period:

> Esther describes her feelings as she is prepared for electroconvulsive therapy: "Then something bent down and took hold of me and shook me like the end of the world. . . . I wondered what terrible thing it was I had done."

4. If you omit a line or more of poetry, or more than one paragraph of prose, use a single line of spaced periods to indicate the omission:

> Scaling little ladders with gluepots and pails of Lysol
>
> . . . .
> Over the weedy acres of your brow

To mend the immense skull-plates and clear
The bald, white tumuli of your eyes.

Punctuate Properly

Punctuation of quotations often causes more trouble than it should. Once again, you just need to keep these simple rules in mind.

1. Periods and commas should be placed inside quotation marks, even if they are not part of the original quotation:

    Buddy offers a helpful suggestion to Esther as she ponders whether city or country life would suit her better: "You could live between them."

    The only exception to this rule is when the quotation is followed by a parenthetical reference. In this case, the period or comma goes after the citation (more on these later in this chapter):

    Buddy's eager response shows his desire to help Esther feel more normal: "You could live between them" (94).

2. Other marks of punctuation—colons, semicolons, question marks, and exclamation points—go outside the quotation marks unless they are part of the original quotation:

    Why is it that when she is with Constantin and the Russian girl Esther feels inadequate and decides, "I had been inadequate all along"?

    Esther realizes her lack of experience and wonders, "How could I compete with that sort of thing?"

Documenting Primary Sources

Unless you are instructed otherwise, you should provide sufficient information for your reader to locate material you quote. Generally, literature papers follow the rules set forth by the Modern Language Association (MLA). These can be found in the *MLA Handbook for Writers of Research Papers* (seventh edition). You should be able to find this book in the reference section of your library. Additionally, its rules for citing both primary and secondary sources are widely available from reputable online sources. One of these is the Online Writing Lab (OWL) at Purdue University. OWL's guide to MLA style is available at http://owl. english.purdue.edu/owl/resource/557/01/. The Modern Language Association also offers answers to frequently asked questions about MLA style on this helpful Web page: http://www.mla.org/style_faq. Generally, when you are citing from literary works in papers, you should keep a few guidelines in mind.

Parenthetical Citations

MLA asks for parenthetical references in your text after quotations. When you are working with prose (short stories, novels, or essays) include page numbers in the parentheses:

> Buddy's eager response shows his desire to help Esther feel more normal: "You could live between them" (94).

When you are quoting poetry, include line numbers:

> Plath's narrator finds some solace as she puts together her father: "Nights, I squat in the cornucopia / Of your left ear, out of the wind, / Counting the red stars and those of plum-color" (24–26).

Works Cited Page

These parenthetical citations are linked to a separate works cited page at the end of the paper. The works cited page lists works alphabetically by the authors' last name. An entry for the above reference to Plath's *The Bell Jar* would read:

> Plath, Sylvia. *The Bell Jar*. 1963. New York: Harper Perennial, 2006. Print.

The *MLA Handbook* includes a full listing of sample entries, as do many of the online explanations of MLA style.

Documenting Secondary Sources

To ensure that your paper is built entirely upon your own ideas and analysis, instructors often ask that you write interpretative papers without any outside research. If, on the other hand, your paper requires research, you must document any secondary sources you use. You need to document direct quotations, summaries or paraphrases of others' ideas, and factual information that is not common knowledge. Follow the guidelines above for quoting primary sources when you use direct quotations from secondary sources. Keep in mind that MLA style also includes specific guidelines for citing electronic sources. OWL's Web site provides a good summary: http://owl.english.purdue.edu/owl/resource/557/09/.

Parenthetical Citations

As with the documentation of primary sources, described above, MLA guidelines require in-text parenthetical references to your secondary sources. Unlike the research papers you might write for a history class, literary research papers following MLA style do not use footnotes as a means of documenting sources. Instead, after a quotation, you should cite the author's last name and the page number:

> "Plath's writing depicts the permeation and poisoning of the human body by toxic chemicals and pollutants; these *material* interpenetrations mirror the ideas of *cultural* movement and permeability that are also important in Plath's work" (Brain 84–85).

If you include the name of the author in your prose, then you would include only the page number in your citation. For example:

> According to Brain, "Plath's writing depicts the permeation and poisoning of the human body by toxic chemicals and pollutants; these *material* interpenetrations mirror the ideas of *cultural* movement and permeability that are also important in Plath's work" (84–85).

If you are including more than one work by the same author, the parenthetical citation should include a shortened yet identifiable version of the title in order to indicate which of the author's works you cite. For example:

> According to Linda Wagner-Martin, "whether because she had found an interesting idiomatic voice or because her prose style had become more inflected, free of the essay tone that was customary for her, it is the rhythmic texture of 'Johnny Panic' that makes it such good writing. It is, in fact, more poem-like than many of Plath's 1959 and 1960 poems" (*Literary Life* 57).

Similarly, and just as important, if you summarize or paraphrase the particular ideas of your source, you must provide documentation:

> The more lively voice in Plath's writing in "Johnny Panic," a departure from her earlier work, helps to create a rhythm and flow in the story that make it more successful than some of the poetry she wrote at this time (Wagner-Martin, *Literary Life* 57).

Works Cited Page
Like the primary sources discussed above, the parenthetical references to secondary sources are keyed to a separate works cited page at the end of your paper. Here is an example of a works cited page that uses the examples cited above. Note that when two or more works by the same author are listed, you should use three hyphens followed by a period in the subsequent entries. You can find a complete list of sample entries in the *MLA Handbook* or from a reputable online summary of MLA style.

WORKS CITED
Anderson, Victoria. "Death Is the Dress She Wears: Plath's Grand Narrative." *Women's Studies* 36 (2007): 79–94. Print.

Badia, Janet. "*The Bell Jar* and Other Prose." *The Cambridge Companion to Sylvia Plath*. Jo Gill, ed. Cambridge: Cambridge U P, 2006. 124–138. Print.

Stevenson, Anne. *Bitter Fame: A Life of Sylvia Plath*. Boston: Houghton Mifflin, 1989. Print.

Plagiarism

Failure to document carefully and thoroughly can leave you open to charges of stealing the ideas of others, which is known as plagiarism, and this is a very serious matter. Remember that it is important to include quotation marks when you use language from your source, even if you use just one or two words. For example, if you wrote, The rhythmic texture of "Johnny Panic" makes it good writing, mainly because Plath found a great idiomatic voice and abandoned the essay style she used so much before, you would be guilty of plagiarism, since you used Wagner-Martin's distinct language without acknowledging her as the source. Instead, you should write something like: Part of what makes "Johnny Panic and the Bible of Dreams" so successful is the "idiomatic voice" Plath uses in the story, making it "more poem-like" than some of the poetry Plath wrote at the time (Wagner-Martin, *Literary Life* 57). In this case, you have properly credited Wagner-Martin.

Similarly, neither summarizing the ideas of an author nor changing or omitting just a few words means that you can omit a citation. Lynda Bundtzen's *Plath's Incarnations* contains the following passage about Plath's motives for writing *The Bell Jar:*

In some ways, Plath's attitude toward *The Bell Jar* while she wrote it is more crucial to an understanding of her life and artistic development than the novel's contents. Her motives for writing *The Bell Jar* are a puzzling combination of financial opportunism and a desire to work through and master her personal history. *Letters Home* shows that Plath is almost always worried about money (as her heroine, Esther, is in the novel) and is particularly beset with financial pressures brought on by her separation from Hughes while preparing *The Bell Jar* for publication. For years, she contemplated the riches of a best-seller and started many novels with the hope of achieving

financial security like that of her benefactor, Olive
Higgins Prouty.

Below are two examples of plagiarized passages:

Plath's motives for writing *The Bell Jar* were probably
largely based on financial concerns. She was often
worried about money, especially when she and her
husband, Ted Hughes, separated. She had dreamed of
publishing a best-selling novel. All of this shows how
important it is to look at Plath's attitude when she
wrote the book and not just the contents of the novel.

Plath's attitude about *The Bell Jar* is crucial to
understanding it. Plath was always worried about money
and was especially worried about money after her
separation from Hughes. She wanted the riches she could
get from writing a best-seller like her benefactor,
Olive Higgins Prouty (Bundtzen 109).

While the first passage does not use Bundtzen's exact language, it lists
the same ideas she says are important to reading Plath without citing
her work. Since this interpretation is Bundtzen's distinct idea, this con-
stitutes plagiarism. The second passage has shortened Bundtzen's passage, changed some wording, and included a citation, but some of the
phrasing is Bundtzen's. The first passage could be fixed with a parenthetical citation. Because some of the wording in the second remains the
same, though, it would require the use of quotation marks, in addition
to a parenthetical citation. The passage below represents an honestly and
adequately documented use of the original passage:

According to Lynda Bundtzen, it is important to consider
what Plath was thinking about *The Bell Jar* while she was
writing it, arguing the author's motives were a "puzzling
combination of financial opportunism and a desire to work
through and master her own personal history" and that she

dreamed of publishing something successful and "achieving financial security like that of her benefactor" (109).

This passage acknowledges that the interpretation is derived from Bundtzen while appropriately using quotations to indicate her precise language.

While it is not necessary to document well-known facts, often referred to as "common knowledge," any ideas or language that you take from someone else must be properly documented. Common knowledge generally includes the birth and death dates of authors or other well-documented facts of their lives. An often-cited guideline is that if you can find the information in three sources, it is common knowledge. Despite this guideline, it is, admittedly, often difficult to know if the facts you uncover are common knowledge or not. When in doubt, document your source.

Sample Essay

Amber Christopher
Mrs. Berg
English II
September 9, 2008

THE TREASON OF ESTHER GREENWOOD
IN SYLVIA PLATH'S *THE BELL JAR*

The theme of treason is a prominent one in Sylvia Plath's *The Bell Jar*. The main character and narrator, Esther Greenwood, opens her story with a flashback of the news stories about Julius and Ethel Rosenberg, famously executed for treason against the United States during the cold war that followed World War II. During the 1950s and 1960s, the cold war was a basically nonviolent battle between communist governments like those of Cuba and the former Soviet Union and democratic governments like those of the United States and England. As readers find out more about Esther, it seems as if she is caught up in her own cold war. By beginning her story with the Rosenbergs' execution by electrocution, Esther illustrates how she feels her own psychiatric treatment (electroconvulsive therapy) was a form of punishment by electrocution. In Esther's own version of cold war, her mother, the main authority figure in her life, becomes the embodiment of what Esther is trying to escape and thus symbolic of what she sees as threatening what she believes in, including her ideas about personal freedom.

Esther's story begins in New York, told in the past tense as she remembers the summer she spent working as an intern at a woman's magazine in the city. It is also the summer she underwent her traumatic electroconvulsive therapy treatment. She starts her recollection with a startling image: "It was a queer, sultry summer, the summer they electrocuted the Rosenbergs. . . . The idea of being electrocuted makes me sick, and that's all there was to read about in the papers" (Plath 1). Esther realizes, "It had nothing to do with me, but I couldn't help wondering what it would be like, being burned alive along all your nerves" (1).

This recollection foreshadows her own experience with electroconvulsive therapy, pointing to her not-so-hidden belief that the treatment she received, with the blessing of her mother, was actually intended to execute her—or at least execute the part of her that refused to obey orders and settle down into the life prescribed for her. When she receives her first electroconvulsive therapy, Esther wonders "what terrible thing it was that I had done" (Plath 143), further indicating she sees what is happening to her as a consequence of a bad act rather than treatment for an illness.

Her association of her treatment with treason and execution helps to highlight the analogy of her relationship with her mother as a war. The two sides of the cold war in Esther's story can be symbolized by Esther and her mother. Like the cold war Plath (and, through her, Esther Greenwood) was living through,

Esther's cold war did not consist so much of open fighting and violent battles; it was more often a battle of ideologies, where one side was trying to convince the world of its superiority over the other's. Mrs. Greenwood's suburban middle-class way of life, the way of life she had in mind for Esther, is epitomized by her as well as by the women who live nearby, like Dodo Conway. Dodo has a degree from Barnard College but stayed home to raise her children; "Everybody loved Dodo. . . . The older people around, like my mother, had two children, and the younger, more prosperous ones had four, but nobody but Dodo was on the verge of a seventh" (Plath 117).

Because she has accepted these sacred duties of motherhood and marriage so thoroughly, Dodo becomes an exceptional woman. That she has embraced social ideologies of marriage and motherhood—the same ideologies against which Esther is fighting—also points to an understanding that there are two sides, one right and one wrong. To Esther, a life like Dodo's seems like a surrender of personal freedom, an imprisonment of sorts. One day while she watches Dodo and her children walk past her house, Esther describes Dodo as wearing "[a] serene, almost religious smile," indicative of her rapture at being a mother so many times over (Plath 116). Esther, on the other hand, declares, "Children made me sick" (Plath 117).

This feeling about children and marriage helps to show the gulf between Esther and social expectations. This gulf also provides further evidence of the cold war between Esther and her mother. Their battle of ideologies comes to light when Mrs. Greenwood, immediately after picking Esther up from her visit to New York, announces the news that Esther was not accepted into a prestigious writing program she had been longing to attend. The nonchalant way in which Mrs. Greenwood delivers the crushing news to her daughter is also indicative of the many ways that she does not understand her daughter and what she values. This difference in values is yet another way that the ideological distance between the two women shows up in the novel.

Esther is not only crushed at the thought of having to stay home, which seems to her not unlike a prison, but she is also angered by the way her mother delivers the news. Esther considers a summer at home with her mother a sentence she must serve, lamenting, "I had never spent a summer in the suburbs before" (Plath 114). It is during this summer that her mother brings her to see Dr. Gordon, who ultimately recommends the electroconvulsive therapy. Esther's mother thinks she has done what is best for her daughter; by trying to make sure Esther fits in and follows the rules, she hopes to make Esther normal, like herself and Dodo, happy to be situated in the suburban middle-class life of wife and mother.

Rather than see her mother's efforts as helpful, though, Esther sees them as punishment for not fitting in. Her inability to conform to societal norms, especially her resistance to marriage and children, becomes the kind of treason that brings on her punishment in the form of electroconvulsive therapy. As she wonders what she did to deserve such treatment, readers are reminded of her fixation with the Rosenbergs and her thoughts about their guilt. Pat Macpherson, writing about *The Bell Jar*, argues that Esther believes the Rosenbergs were "scapegoated as spies, Communists, traitors in our midst, with their Jewishness and Ethel Rosenberg's strong womanhood seen as part of the Alien nature of this Enemy Within" (2).

This idea of the Rosenbergs as scapegoats shows that when the status quo is being threatened, it is important to have examples that reinforce the ideals and also demonstrate what happens to those who threaten those ideals. Because she refuses to embrace the lifestyle of her mother and other middle-class women of the era, Esther has committed treason—she exhibits that "Alien nature" Macpherson notes and thus must be apprehended and punished before she undermines the fabric of the culture against which she rebels.

Esther's distress at the fate of the Rosenbergs mimics her misgivings about what her life might have in store for her if she follows the path society has set in front of her: "Esther's personal horror at what she finds in life is set against the horror of their executions" (Wagner-Martin 186). Much of what she sees as horrifying in her life is, as Esther views it, caused by her mother. There are many images throughout the book that help to show how Esther sees her mother as the enemy, as a force against which she must do battle. One night as she listens to her mother snoring while she sleeps, she becomes increasingly irritated by the sound and thinks, "for a while it seemed to me that the only way to stop it would be to take the column of skin and sinew from which it rose and twist it to silence between my hands" (Plath 123). This hint at violence against her mother points to Esther's sense of her mother as a danger to her rather than as a comfort; at times the mere presence of her mother seems like an almost mortal threat.

Feeding into these feelings that she needs to eliminate the enemy that is her mother, Esther sees her mother's insistence that she conform to the typical middle-class lifestyle as a threat to her freedom. She does not want to be like her mother and Dodo Conway. When she is not accepted to the writing workshop, it is as if she had tried to escape to freedom but was foiled. She wants to be a poet, not a housewife and mother; she remembers Buddy Willard telling her menacingly that once she was married and a mother, "I wouldn't want to write poems any more" and thinks to herself, "maybe it was true that when you were married and had children is was like being brainwashed, and afterward you went about numb as a slave in some private, totalitarian state" (Plath 85). Esther gets a taste of this totalitarian state when she is forced to spend the summer basically living her mother's life; she takes it as a sentence rather than a comfort. Esther is intent on keeping her freedom and not becoming part of that "totalitarian state," but in many ways, she is now a prisoner of the other side since her chance at freedom—the writing program—has been taken away. When she cannot be "controlled" and made to follow the rules of society, to join that state, the punishment for such failure to follow the rules is electrocution in the form of electroconvulsive therapy.

The suspicion of Esther's refusal to conform and the "execution" she undergoes because of that refusal to embrace the ideology of her mother are other elements of the cold war between the two women. The cold war is a powerful comparison to use in Esther's story because it was a battle of ideologies rather than a physical war. Even without an actual armed conflict, the threat was always there; a psychological battle was always going on. This is the kind of war Esther Greenwood is engaged in. Each side is wary of the other, just waiting. Esther seemed to be on her mother's side, getting good grades throughout school, going to college, getting the prestigious internship in New York, but then she showed she was not truly a member of the party, a supporter of the cause, and had to be punished.

In essence, the "electrocution" Esther underwent killed the part of her that was rebelling because in the present, when she is telling the story, she has presumably accepted the life that she fought against. She looks back on the experience in New York with a new kind of reality, as if realizing her folly at taking it so seriously: "I got such a kick out of all those free gifts showering on to us. For a long time afterward I hid them away, but later, when I was all right again, I brought them out" (Plath 3). She has obviously overcome her aversion to children, though, because she notes, "last week I cut the plastic starfish off the sunglass case for the baby to play with" (Plath 3). So now she has rejoined the group, she has been brought back to the fold. Since she refers to "the baby" and "the house," it can be assumed she is now the middle-class wife and mother that she so dreaded becoming before her therapy.

By framing her own experiences with the execution of the Rosenbergs, Esther shows her preoccupation with their situation. She does not really protest the executions, but she does immediately show a degree of solidarity with them as she talks about how awful it would be to be "burned alive" (Plath 1). This ambiguity about the Rosenbergs and their fate shows Esther's ambiguity about her own situation. At the end of the book, she contemplates being released from the treatment center, thinking "I had hoped, at my departure, I would feel sure and knowledgeable about everything that lay ahead—after all, I had been 'analyzed.' Instead, all I could see were question marks" (Plath 243). In the end, it seems that Esther's mother's side—the side that demanded treatment for Esther to make her more like Mrs. Greenwood and Dodo—has won. Yet as much as it appears Esther has been won over, there is still some doubt about where her allegiances truly lie, even in her own mind.

WORKS CITED

Macpherson, Pat. *Reflecting on* The Bell Jar. London: Routledge, 1991. Print.

Plath, Sylvia. *The Bell Jar.* New York: Harper Perennial, 2006. Print.

Wagner-Martin, Linda. *Sylvia Plath: A Biography.* New York: Simon and Schuster, 1987. Print.

HOW TO WRITE
ABOUT SYLVIA PLATH

Sylvia Plath was born on October 27, 1932, to Otto and Aurelia Plath, who lived in Jamaica Plain, Massachusetts, a suburb of Boston. Her brother, Warren, was born in 1935. Plath's parents were each of German heritage, a fact that is referenced in much of Plath's writing. Her father, who had emigrated from Germany to the United States in 1901 when he was 16, learned English and attended college, becoming a professor of entomology (the study of insects) whose area of specialty was bees. Plath's mother, Aurelia Schober, was studying for her master's degree at Boston University when she met Otto Plath, a man many years her senior. The two were married in January 1932. Plath's father died when she was eight years old from complications related to diabetes. Her mother was loath to let her children see her grieve, so his death went largely unmourned in young Sylvia's mind. Sylvia went on to attend Smith College in Massachusetts and then studied abroad at Cambridge University, where she met fellow poet Ted Hughes. The two were married in 1956 and had two children, Frieda, born in 1960, and Nicholas, born in 1962. In late 1962, Plath discovered her husband was having an affair with a mutual friend of the couple, and the marriage began to fall apart. On February 10, 1963, Sylvia Plath was found dead in the apartment she shared with her children. She had taken sleeping pills and, famously, placed her head in the gas oven.

For most readers, this story is not unfamiliar, meaning for many the most significant thing about reading Sylvia Plath's work is that it somehow foreshadows her suicide. Because her death is so famous, perhaps even more so than her life, it is an almost irresistible temptation. However, in order to truly appreciate Plath's work, it is crucial to set aside that tendency to read it only in terms of her death. As biographer Lynda Bundtzen argues, "the circumstances of her death have been crucial in shaping response to her work and in contributing to the overall estimate of her imagination as morbidly attracted to death" (159). Linda Wagner-Martin agrees, stating, "The temptation to . . . re-create Plath's biography through readings of her work—and, implicitly, to try to unearth the complex reasons for her tragic suicide—overtakes the most focused reader" (*Literary Life* 133). Thus as you begin to read and write about the works of Sylvia Plath, it is important to maintain a certain amount of objectivity, to make an attempt to suspend your awareness of that tragic suicide and read the work as that of a writer who *lived* rather than that of a writer who ended her own life.

One way to do that is to consider how Plath incorporated her life into her work. Plath was intent on using her own experiences in her writing in all genres; Bundtzen notes that it is this determination to use those experiences that likely contributes to readers' tendencies to read Plath's work as largely autobiographical: "One possible source of critical misrepresentation is Plath's determination to speak of larger issues through the particulars of experience" (159). In other words, Plath's idea that basing her writing on her experiences so that her message would seem more real and relatable to readers was correct.

Unfortunately, though, because readers are so familiar with Plath's personal history, they often do not recognize that she is not merely recounting her life but is usually offering serious commentary on issues that are important to her.

In order to gain an understanding of Plath's work as not mere autobiography, it can be useful to think of the difference between inspiration and documentation. It is perhaps more appropriate to think of Plath's experiences as inspiration for her writing rather than considering her writing as documentation of her experiences. In the introduction to a collection of Plath's short stories published after her death, *Johnny Panic and the Bible of Dreams,* Ted Hughes cites his wife's own words: "'My life may at last get into my writing'" (Plath, *Johnny Panic* 4); he follows up by agreeing with her, writing, "The material of these stories . . . is basically description of first-hand experience" (Plath, *Johnny Panic* 6). Plath, however, was careful to point out that her work was not simply autobiography, as Bundtzen argues. She declared in a BBC interview, "I think that personal experience is very important, but certainly it shouldn't be a kind of shut-box and mirror-looking, narcissistic experience. I believe it should be relevant, and relevant to the larger things, the bigger things" (qtd. in Annas 12). Keeping this in mind while reading Plath's work can help you discover a much wider variety of topics about which to write.

Another way to approach reading Plath's work is to envision her not as a distressed woman writing about her impending doom but rather as a talented young writer trying to make a name for herself in the literary world and eager for financial success as a writer, as well. Hughes writes of Plath:

> She declared her ambition about two things. The first was to become a proficient story writer, of the high-power practical, popular American type, whose stories could appear in the big journals and earn huge sums of cash and give her the feeling of being a professional with a real job in the real world. The second was to become a proficient freelance journalist, who could wander about the world and finance her adventures by writing about them. (2)

For those who see her as a martyr, imagining Plath as someone pursuing money and fame for her work can be jarring. But while earning a handsome living and becoming famous were undeniably important to Plath, she was intent that those desires not take over her writing. In her journals, she writes about writing, "You do not do it first for money. Money isn't why you sit down at the typewriter. Not that you don't want it. It is only too lovely when a profession pays for your bread and butter" (Kukil 436).

The struggle to achieve fame and fortune yet remain true to her ideals was one that Plath would experience throughout her career. She sent poems and stories to many magazines, including *Ladies' Home Journal*, which she in one journal entry scorns for some of the featured articles (Kukil 361) but is a few days later excited when the magazine accepts one of her poems for what she calls a "pleasantly lucrative" sum (Kukil 365). In a letter to her mother, she complains of what she calls her "awful first ladies' magazine story," saying it was "very stiff and amateurish"

(Plath, *Letters Home* 436). In that same letter she was delighted that *The New Yorker* had accepted her poems "Tulips" and "Blackberrying," further demonstrating her desire to achieve both commercial and critical success.

Another area where Plath received some critical success was in the visual arts. Because she is so well known for her poetry and her lone published novel, it is often a surprise for readers to find out that she was an avid visual artist as well. As a young girl, she often drew pictures to accompany her writing. One excellent resource to see much of Plath's visual art is the book *Eye Rhymes: Sylvia Plath's Art of the Visual*. As Susan Gubar points out in this book, "Unquestionably Plath made the right decision when she relinquished her ambition in the sister art of painting so as to dedicate herself to her poetic gift. But the verse cannot be fully appreciated without some knowledge of the drawings, cutouts, and portraits" (232). The *Christian Science Monitor* even published two of Plath's illustrated articles, works that "offered an artist's perspective on the sights she drew"; Kathleen Connors argues that Plath, "As always . . . considered the act of creating art and her subject matter equally worthy of analysis" (130). As you begin to write about Plath's work, consider how this knowledge about her skills in drawing and painting affects how you read her writing. How do you see her appreciation of the visual arts in the language and the images she creates in her writing? Think about how you might be able to include some discussion about Plath's work in this media in a project about her writing.

Her Influences

Perhaps because of her life story, including her suicide, Sylvia Plath and her work have inspired myriad writers to pay homage to her. In her book, *The Plath Cabinet*, Catherine Bowman writes:

> These inklings, riffs, and big-picture imaginings celebrate, investigate, and improvise on the life and work of Sylvia Plath. They are based on her published and unpublished work, as well as hearsay and real-life events. . . . This book was a way for me to get to know Sylvia Plath. (69)

As you read through Plath's works, and as you read through this book, think about what it is about Plath's work that inspires this sort of devotion and emulation. Consider finding other works that are modeled on or inspired by Sylvia Plath's life and writing as a way to measure the lasting effect her work has on writers. What can you identify about Plath's writing and her story that makes her so popular as a conduit through which people can create their own works?

Further evidence of Plath's ongoing influence can be seen in popular culture. Popular culture references to Plath are common, even decades after her death. Often her work, especially *The Bell Jar*, is shown in the hands of a troubled young woman, seeming to underscore or imply that the young woman reading it is, indeed, troubled. In the movie *10 Things I Hate about You* (1999), a retelling of Shakespeare's *Taming of the Shrew*, the main character, Kat, is shown reading *The Bell Jar*. She is "the stereotypical Plath reader, representing the generation of bright, troubled young women" drawn to Plath's writing, and especially the story of Esther Greenwood (Smith). *The Bell Jar* also shows up in the movie *Heathers*, which Nick Adams sees as providing the film's villain, J.D., with his "initial inspiration to turn [one of the] Heather's murder into a suicide" (Burns). More recently, the animated sitcom *Family Guy* featured *The Bell Jar* in an episode where Meg Griffin, the hapless only daughter of the family, is crying in her bedroom. Her mother responds by laying a bottle of sleeping pills and a copy of *The Bell Jar* on Meg's bed, saying "whatever happens, happens." As you think about topics for papers and projects, you might want to begin by asking why Plath's work is so often portrayed this way. There are numerous examples of Plath's work being featured in films and television; reviewing some of those might give you an idea for a paper.

These representations of Plath and her work in popular culture, including the biopic *Sylvia*, also help to illustrate the many different things Plath represents for readers. For some, she highlights the difficulties faced by women as they try to juggle their desires for professional success with expectations for their domestic success. For others, she serves as an example of what was wrong with the system for treating mental illness. Still others see her as an archetype of the tortured writer. Many critics wonder if these views of Plath would change had she not committed suicide. As you start on a writing project about Plath and/or her works, it could be useful to apply several different tactics for reading Plath to one work and explore how those different approaches to her work intersect. You might also ask yourself some questions about whether her work would have achieved the kind of commercial and critical success it has had her career not been cut short.

Plath's daughter, Frieda Hughes, expresses some anger at the way her mother's life and work have been co-opted by readers and critics over the years: "[T]he point of anguish at which my mother killed herself was taken over by strangers, possessed and reshaped by them" (xiv). She laments, "Since she died my mother has been dissected, analyzed, reinterpreted, reinvented, fictionalized, and in some cases completely fabricated. It comes down to this: her own words describe her best" (xvii). Kathleen Connors agrees, noting that, while there is some merit to reading Plath's work as an indication of her suicidal thoughts, readers should use caution when doing so; "While this interpretation has foundation, it may be more of a reading in hindsight instead of planning on Plath's part" (135).

Reading through several critical interpretations of Plath's work could help put the realities of her life and the conditions surrounding the creation of her work into perspective and help you decide on a topic for a paper as well. Almost any writer you read and write about will be the subject of many different interpretations, yet some spark more passionate debate than others. Again, it will likely be useful for you to think about why Plath's work is so closely identified with her death, as her daughter points out. You might also consider whether you see one or more of these critical interpretations of Plath's work or of a particular work as more accurate or fair than others and why you believe that to be the case.

Her Work

Sylvia Plath is perhaps best known for her only published novel, *The Bell Jar,* but she is also widely recognized for her poetry. Plath did, however, also write short stories, essays, and even a poem meant to be read as a play. Her work clearly deals with many personal concerns, but it also addresses major social and political issues. This book will introduce you to several of Plath's works as well as give you ideas for working with her writing in your own essays and projects. The following sections will offer discussion of some of the important themes in Plath's work; the characters she creates in her writing; some of the guiding philosophies in her work; how she worked in a variety of genres; and notable images, language, and symbols in Plath's works.

Themes

War, especially the aftermath of World War II and the cold war, is a recurring theme in Plath's work. In 1961, she expresses concern about the cold war, writing to her mother, "I've been very gloomy about the bomb news. . . . The fallout-shelter craze in America sounds mad. Well, I would rather be in Devon, where I am in the country, than anywhere else right now" (Kukil 434). In another letter written later that year, she writes that she is losing sleep over "all the warlike talk in the papers" and the angry exchanges between U.S. president John F. Kennedy and Soviet premier Nikita Kruschev; she is also upset by some American policies; "I am also horrified at the U.S. selling missiles (without warheads) to Germany, awarding former German officers medals" (Kukil 438). Plath's concern with what she saw going on in the world around her, including disappointment in the United States and England for their actions, comes through in much of her work. In *The Bell Jar* she begins the story with Esther Greenwood's recollection of the execution of Julius and Ethel Rosenberg for treason against the United States. The execution sparked a great deal of controversy both in the United States and abroad. In poems like "Daddy" and "Lady Lazarus," references to World War II, and especially the Holocaust, are obvious.

Death, perhaps as an expression of this fear about the fate of the world, is another prominent theme in Plath's work. She discusses suicide obviously in *The Bell Jar* through Esther Greenwood's experiences, and she also references attempts at suicide in "Lady Lazarus" and "Daddy." The death of her father affected Sylvia Plath profoundly and is widely considered to have played a role in her own suicide attempts. These feelings about death are often reflected in images of darkness and despair in Plath's work, especially in her poetry. If you choose to write about death as a theme in Plath's work, think about moving beyond the obvious (merely identifying instances where death is referenced) and addressing what Plath is saying about life and death through those images and references. Rather than using the images of death in Plath's work as a way to foretell her suicide, think about what she might be saying about life and how the constant presence of death affects how people live.

Interestingly, although death is a common theme in her work, rebirth is an equally important theme to consider when reading Plath's works. Even when a character seems to want to die, the act of dying (especially through attempts at suicide) results in a transformation into life, such as in *The Bell Jar;* "Its outcome was to be positive: the rebirth of Esther, a woman who had come through both Dante's hell and her own, to find her fulfillment . . . in herself" (Wagner-Martin, *Biography* 187). In "Lady Lazarus" and "Ariel," the speakers in the poem become stronger figures after they have, in a sense, lived through death and are triumphant in their rebirth. In "Johnny Panic and the Bible of Dreams," the narrator is reborn when she is saved by the godlike Johnny Panic; rather than panicking at what seems to be her impending doom, she is calmed by a sense of being born again. As you consider writing about this theme in Plath's work, think about how death is defeated and turned into rebirth. You might also want to consider Wagner-Martin's point and decide whether Plath consistently portrays rebirth as positive or if she is doubtful about it. What religious overtones are there in the portrayals of rebirth in Plath's works?

An additional theme to look for in Plath's works is the struggle of women to find a balance between societal expectations of them and their own goals. This is a central theme in *The Bell Jar* as Esther Greenwood deals with pressures from her mother and other characters (like Buddy Willard) to get married and start a family despite her interest in becoming a professional writer. Poems like "Ariel" and "Lady Lazarus" also reflect Plath's feelings about what society expects of women. The poem for three voices, "Three Women," illustrates three different feelings women might have about being a wife and mother. If you decide to pursue this theme for an essay, you should consider thinking about what Plath is saying about the issue. Do you think she is calling for action? Rather than assuming she is making sweeping statements about women, think about what she might be saying about cultural expectations for both men and women.

Characters

Since much of Plath's work was poetry, writing about characters in her work can seem daunting. Plath's novel, *The Bell Jar,* and her short stories, like "Johnny Panic and the Bible of Dreams" offer more clear opportunities to discuss character. Esther Greenwood is arguably the most famous character Plath created and is often seen as a kind of alter ego for Plath, especially since Esther's experiences are so closely related to the author's own. As you decide on a topic for an essay or other project, beware of seeing the characters in Plath's work solely as incarnations of Plath herself. Plath was careful to point out the importance of connecting personal experience in one's writing to something bigger. When you read through Plath's work to find a character or characters to write about, this idea can prove useful.

As you decide on an appropriate topic dealing with character in Plath's work, think about current events at the times Plath was writing the works. How do the characters' feelings and actions relate to important issues of the time? Many critics see Plath's work as part of the feminist literary canon; you might want to explore the ways in which Esther Greenwood reflects feminist ideals or how her experiences illustrate the struggles of young women in the 1950s and 1960s. Other critics see Plath as making strong statements about treatment for mental illness. What does the narrator in "Johnny Panic and the Bible of Dreams" have to say about this issue? Consider how Plath's experiences reflect her views on this issue.

Although they remain nameless, the three women in the poem/play "Three Women" are characters that offer a great deal of material for an essay. As you read through the piece, analyze how Plath creates three distinct voices for the characters. You might also want to think about how these three characters complement the voices of other characters in Plath's work. Are they reiterating points made by Esther Greenwood or by the narrator in "Johnny Panic and the Bible of Dreams"? You could also consider how Plath creates characters out of speakers and narrators of her poetry; rather than thinking that the speakers of her poems are all Plath herself, think about how she crafts characters with distinct voices in her poetry. What does the character say about an issue? How does Plath use those distinct voices of her characters to address something bigger than just her own life experiences?

History and Context

One important thing to keep in mind as you read Plath's works and prepare to write about them is just how much of Plath's work has been published posthumously, including many pieces that she most likely did not intend to be published since she did not send them out herself. Ted Hughes writes of the pieces in the collection *Johnny Panic and the Bible of Dreams*, "Sylvia Plath herself had certainly rejected several of the stories here, so they are printed against her better judgment. That must be taken into account. But in spite of the obvious weaknesses, they seem interesting enough to keep, if only as notes toward her inner autobiography" (7). Many readers and critics argue that it is unfair to judge work that Plath never intended to be seen by the general public. Hughes urges readers to keep that in mind: "Reading this collection, it should be remembered that her reputation rests on the poems of her last six months" (9). As you decide on topics for essays, you might want to think about the clear distinction between what Plath intended to be read and what she did not. There is much of Plath's personal writing available to read, including her journals. How would you describe the difference between Plath's private voice and her public voice?

The voice Plath uses in her work is often considered her own, especially by readers who are familiar with her death. Knowing more about literary movements at the time Plath was writing might help to dispel some of those ideas, however. Plath was excited by the work of American poets in the late 1950s and early 1960s; she had studied under Robert Lowell, studied with Anne Sexton, and admired Adrienne Rich and other poets who populated what is usually referred to as the confessional poetry movement (Wagner-Martin, *Literary Life* 134). Although she did not label herself a confessional poet, Plath was drawn to the personal tone of the works of this group. She saw what they were doing as new and exciting, especially "'inwardness of [their] images, their plummeting subjectivity'" (qtd. in Wagner-Martin, *Literary Life* 134–35). Her appreciation of this technique offers another way to look at the personal voice in her poetry— not just Plath reciting her own experiences but experimenting with new ways to write about issues germane to others, as well. As you think about paper topics, you might want to research the confessional movement and decide how (or even whether) Plath's work fits into that genre.

Philosophy and Ideas

Plath's own words offer unique insight into her philosophies about writing and also help readers see some of the things she was passionate enough about to address in her writing. Especially when reading through the drafts of poems in the collection *Ariel* and in reading through her letters to her mother and brother in *Letters Home,* it becomes clear that death was something that Plath thought about often. Too often, though, when readers (especially first-time readers who are largely familiar with Plath because of her famous suicide) confront her work they immediately pick up on the images of death and assume they foreshadow her decision to take her own life. What is dangerous about that, though, is that it can make readers a little lazy; by automatically connecting her writing with her suicide, readers miss out on a lot of richly wrought poetry and fiction. In the biographical information about Plath, including her own journals and letters, readers can see that Plath was concerned about things such as the environment, political issues, war (including the cold war), civil rights, and myriad other issues. Her novel, *The Bell Jar,* illustrates her concern with many of these issues as enacted and embodied in the struggles of Esther Greenwood.

Plath's work also illustrates some of her feelings about marriage and motherhood. In *The Bell Jar,* Buddy Willard tells Esther Greenwood that once she becomes a wife and mother she will no longer want to be a poet, and she wonders if that is true, thinking it would be like living in a "totalitarian state" (85). In "Lady Lazarus," Plath's woman speaker describes being on display, like a possession. In "Three Women," the three voices speak of three different experiences of becoming a mother (not all of them happy), highlighting the fact that motherhood is not always welcome for every woman. Plath herself had worried about marriage, but she felt that with her husband, Ted Hughes, she had found someone who would appreciate her as a writer and an equal. Thinking about these issues in a broad way can help you decide on essay topics. You might address Plath's work as feminist literature by exploring the statements she makes about marriage and motherhood. You could also argue that Plath's work reveres motherhood; she wrote several poems about motherhood, including "Nick and the Candlestick" and "Morning Song," that can be read as her appreciation of becoming a mother.

Form and Genre

Plath most often referred to herself as a poet, and the bulk of the work she submitted for publication was poetry. Her only completed novel, *The Bell*

Jar, is probably the work she is most famous for though. She wrote short stories, the best known of which is "Johnny Panic and the Bible of Dreams," produced in 1958 and inspired by a clerical job she had at the psychiatric ward of a hospital. The poem "Three Women" has been produced as a play because it was written for three voices, but there is no evidence that Plath ever really considered herself a playwright. Throughout her career she also wrote nonfiction essays for magazines and other publications as well. The fact that she wrote in a variety of genres and was also a gifted visual artist speaks to her versatility as a writer and also to her ambition to get her work published. One idea for a paper might be to read critical reviews of Plath's work in different genres and decide which of the genres was best suited to her or which of the genres readers and critics are drawn to most strongly.

One thing that Plath was insistent on was the utility of reading her poetry out loud. She felt that it was important to understanding the work; in an interview with Peter Orr for the BBC, Plath read several of her works, making a case for "her comment that these poems were written for the ear rather than the eye, and that she said them aloud to herself as she wrote them" (Wagner-Martin, *Biography* 224). There are numerous online recordings available of Plath reading her poems; as you consider which poem or poems to write about for an essay, you might want to consider listening to them to address this idea of Plath's. How does hearing her read her work out loud change how you, as a reader, understand the work? What changes when you get the emphases from Plath rather than providing them yourself?

Especially in *The Bell Jar,* Plath's writing is often epistolary, meaning the story is told through letters, newspaper clippings, and diary entries; think of how Joan helps to tell the story of Esther's suicide through the newspaper clippings she saved and how Esther often refers to newspaper headlines about the Rosenberg execution and other issues she finds disturbing or interesting. As you read through Plath's work, consider this idea and how you might be able to write about the epistolary nature of many of Plath's works. Where do you see her incorporating other bits of writing into a poem or short story? How does that reinforce the point she is making in the work?

Language, Symbols, and Imagery

Nature images are a common feature in Sylvia Plath's writing; she was often inspired by her surroundings, including the environment in which she lived. This interest in the natural explains many of the images that regularly show up in Plath's work; the moon is a recurring figure in Plath's work, especially her poetry. The so-called 1961 poems, which were written after her breakup with husband Ted Hughes, are especially known for their references to the moon. Those references are often centered on the feminine in some way, either by association with a specific woman (the moon in "The Moon and the Yew Tree" is symbolic of her mother) or by association with things related to motherhood (as in "Edge" and "Childless Woman").

Trees and flowers are other commonly featured images in Plath's work. In *The Bell Jar*, Esther's dream of sitting in a fig tree and trying to decide which fruit to pick is extremely significant because it points to the dilemma she faces in determining what to do with her future. The tree becomes symbolic of the issues she faced as a young woman during the 1950s and 1960s when women's roles were a source of much debate. One of Plath's most critically acclaimed poems, "The Moon and the Yew Tree," was inspired by a scene she and her husband saw across the street from their house in Devon (Wagner-Martin, *Biography* 195). Plath's home in Devon was in the country, which meant she was surrounded by flora and fauna; many of her poems, including "Tulips" and "Poppies in July," were inspired by the natural world around her. As you consider writing about images of nature in Plath's work, remember that she lived in both the country and the city; do you see more nature images emerging in the poetry written while she lived in Devon than when she lived in metropolitan areas?

Nature images that are reflective of her father and his presence, or lack of presence, in her life can be seen in Plath's bee poems. Since her father's specialty as an entomologist was bumblebees, the fact that she writes about bees and beekeeping in several of her poems points to her continuing efforts to reconnect with her father after his death. The yew tree in the poem "The Moon and the Yew Tree" is symbolic of her father, a dark, mute figure that she is unable to decipher.

Darkness is another image that recurs in Plath's poetry, especially. In poems like "Ariel" and "Blackberrying," the dark colors of berries are described. Darkness also symbolizes searching in many of Plath's works. "The speaker's search for truth is one theme that dominates Plath's Devon poems. . . . It quickly became one of her strongest, most surprising and most intense poems. . . . Images of blackness, fear, and hopelessness occur in many of Plath's 1961 poems" (Wagner-Martin, *Biography* 195). In some cases, her use of darkness is used as a contrast to light. This can be seen as a verbal version of the artistic technique of chiaroscuro, putting dark and light in direct contrast with each other. Plath's background in the visual arts likely influenced her in the creation of images in her writing, especially in her poetry. As you search for paper topics, you might wish to find some images of Plath's sketches and paintings to see how they influence your own reading of her written work and whether you can equate her artistry in the visual arts with her artistry in the literary arts.

Plath's use of language is often startling. Specific language referring to the Holocaust, including her use of German words in her poems, occurs in several works but perhaps most notably in "Daddy." She carefully chooses line breaks in her poetry to emphasize specific words and images as well. Plath uses language economically; rather than lengthy descriptions, she chooses specific words to create an image or evoke a certain feeling in her readers. Her decisions about language use in her poems might also explain her views on the importance of reading them out loud; reading them makes those choices in language even more apparent and all the more powerful for readers as they become listeners.

Plath's writing was also undoubtedly influenced by her treatment for depression. Images of electricity are prominent in *The Bell Jar* and "Johnny Panic and the Bible of Dreams" as the heroine in each is subjected to electroconvulsive therapy, as Plath herself had been. "Lady Lazarus" also includes strong images of burning and ash, likely also references to the therapy. In "Daddy," Plath references attempted suicide and the resulting efforts to put the speaker back together again. The poem "Three Women" contains a number of references to the range of common symbols Plath frequently employed. It might be useful as you think about a paper topic to isolate a few poems from a particular period or isolate a particular image that interests you and look for instances of it in a few of Plath's poems.

As you consider writing about symbolism in Plath's work, beware of oversimplifying those symbols. As Lynda Bundtzen points out of the poems "Edge" and "The Moon and the Yew Tree," for example, "It is not particularly useful . . . to codify symbols in either poem (i.e., fire means this, the moon means that). . . . If there is a specific meaning to either poem, it is in the complexion of the mind, the emotions of the speaker, and Plath's deft transference of these feelings to her reader" (203). It might be more useful in some cases, as Bundtzen argues, to consider how the symbolism affects readers rather than speculate about Plath's motives for including it in the work or works you are examining.

Compare and Contrast

Since Plath wrote in more than one genre, comparing and contrasting images and characters in those different genres, especially *The Bell Jar*, could prove fruitful as you plan a writing project. You could think about how the narrator in "Johnny Panic and the Bible of Dreams" compares to Esther Greenwood in *The Bell Jar*. Consider how the speaker in "Lady Lazarus" is similar to the speaker in "Ariel." Although Plath was still a young woman when she died, there is a great deal of her work available to readers; as you think about writing a compare and contrast essay, you might want to look at an early piece and one of the last pieces she wrote and analyze her growth as a writer as reflected in those pieces. Since there is a restored edition of the collection *Ariel* available (which includes a foreword from her daughter, Frieda Hughes), you could also compare the original versions of the poems, some including her own notes, to the final version that was published. Looking for changes that reflect some influences from her earlier works could offer you some viable ideas for papers.

Another opportunity for compare and contrast essays about Plath is to analyze some of the biographies written about her. Authors have taken a variety of approaches to writing about Plath's life and death, and there is debate over the validity of some of those works. By reading through the acknowledgments and/or preface material in the biographies, you can determine that some were written with the support and assistance of the Plath estate. Some authors have worked closely with the Plath archives at the Lilly Library at Indiana University and at Smith College. Others look at Plath's mental illness, examining her life and death through her treatment for depression and suicide attempts. Find biographies that take different approaches to discussing Plath's life and work and chart a compare and contrast essay based on them; you might consider whether any one seems more sympathetic or more critical of Plath and why you think that might be. Which would you deem most reliable, and why?

One more vein you can mine for compare and contrast essays is the marriage of Plath and Ted Hughes. Since Hughes was also a poet, and a more famous and successful one while he and Plath were married, examining works by both of them could provide rich material for compare and contrast essays. Hughes and Plath often discussed poetry, and as biographer Paul Alexander points out, even as Plath became more successful, "Ted continued to exert an influence over Plath's creative work. As she tapped into her subconscious through mental exercises which Ted showed her how to do . . . she opened herself up to write more innovative—and better—poetry" (266–67). To examine this influence, you could choose an image that shows up in each of the poets' works, like trees (such as Plath's "The Moon and the Yew Tree" and Hughes's "The Laburnum Top"). You might find a useful topic by comparing works by the two poets written around the same time or even by looking at work by Hughes published after his wife's death; do you see her influencing his work?

Finally, since there are so many writers who claim they are inspired by Plath, you could look at work by one or more of them (like Catherine Bowman's *The Plath Cabinet*) and prepare a compare and contrast essay in which you look for that inspiration. Read through a work inspired by Plath and look for specific images or word choices that you see as obviously referring to Plath. You might also find similarities in the formation of stanzas or lines in poems that are clearly derived from Plath's structures. Consider the difference in the times in which each piece was written as well. For instance, if you read something that was written a whole generation after Plath's work, how might you see some of the same themes being brought up or some of the images from Plath's work used in a new context to appeal to readers of a different generation?

Final Words

As Tracy Brain argues, there is what she sees as a formula that is commonly used when reading Plath's works: "Speakers of poems can be assumed to be Plath herself, instead of literary characters. . . . The facts of Plath's life are what the poetry is about. . . . In turn, the poetry causes the life, or rather, the death. . . . The premise is that to explain the life, readers can look at the work. Reciprocally, to explain the work, they can turn to the life" (20). While there are undeniably some good reasons to look at Plath's life to explain her work and vice versa, it will help you, as a reader and a writer, to see past this formula and analyze Plath's work as you would other works; see narrators as carefully designed characters, settings as purposeful creations, and the writing as specifically crafted to make serious points and evoke specific responses from readers.

Bibliography and Online Resources for "How to Write about Sylvia Plath"

10 Things I Hate About You. Dir. Gil Junger. Touchstone. 1999.

Alexander, Paul. *Rough Magic: A Biography of Sylvia Plath.* New York: DeCapo, 1999. Print.

Annas, Pamela J. *A Disturbance in Mirrors: The Poetry of Sylvia Plath.* New York: Greenwood P, 1988. Print.

Bowman, Catherine. *The Plath Cabinet.* New York: Four Way Books, 2009.

Brain, Tracy. *The Other Sylvia Plath.* Harlow, England: Pearson, 2001. Print.

Bundtzen, Lynda. *Plath's Incarnations: Woman and the Creative Process.* Ann Arbor, MI: U of Michigan P, 1983. Print.

Burns, Nick. "*Heathers:* Scent of Dominance." *Jump Cut: A Review of Contemporary Media* May 1991. Web. 16 June 2010.

Connors, Kathleen. "Living Color: The Interactive Arts of Sylvia Plath." *Eye Rhymes: Sylvia Plath's Art of the Visual.* Kathleen Connors and Sally Bayley, Eds. Oxford: Oxford U P, 2007. Print.

Hughes, Frieda. Foreword. ix–xvii. Plath, Sylvia. *Ariel.* Restored ed. London: Faber and Faber, 2004. Print.

Hughes, Ted. Introduction. 1–9. 1996. Plath, Sylvia. *Johnny Panic and the Bible of Dreams.* New York: Harper, 2000. Print.

Kukil, Karen V. *The Unabridged Journals of Sylvia Plath.* New York: Anchor, 2000. Print.

Plath, Sylvia. *The Bell Jar.* 1963. New York: Harper Collins, 1971. Print.

———. *Letters Home.* Ed. Aurelia Plath. New York: Harper and Row, 1975. Print.

Smith, Rosi. "Seeing Through the Bell Jar: Distorted Female Identity in Cold War America." aspeers.com. aspeers, 2008. Web. 17 June 2010.

"Stew-Roids." *Family Guy.* Perf. Mila Kunis. Fox. 26 Apr. 2009. Television.

Wagner-Martin, Linda. *Sylvia Plath: A Literary Life.* Hampshire, England: Macmillan P, 1999. Print.

———. *Sylvia Plath: A Biography.* New York: Simon and Schuster, 1987. Print.

"JOHNNY PANIC AND THE BIBLE OF DREAMS"

READING TO WRITE

"Johnny Panic and the Bible of Dreams" is one of Sylvia Plath's many short stories, many of which were written in the 1950s, early on in her writing career and before she achieved fame for her poetry. Of those stories, this is perhaps the best known. Since Plath is obviously well known and critically acclaimed for her poetry and for her lone novel, *The Bell Jar,* many readers are surprised to find out that she wrote numerous short stories. "Johnny Panic and the Bible of Dreams" was written in December 1958, when Plath was living in Boston. The story has its roots in clerical work she did at Massachusetts General Hospital in Boston. As one biographer notes, in this story "Plath sees the dreams people have, the specific forms of their potential madness, as a more accurate index to them than is their social behavior" (Annas 119). Plath herself thought "she had at last got her life into her writing" in this story (Stevenson 142). Shades of her own experience with psychiatric treatment are evident in the story, although it is doubtful the story is entirely autobiographical; rather, it could be more fruitful to read this story as an exercise in which Plath flexes her muscles as a writer. In her journals, Plath writes of her hopefulness about "Johnny Panic and the Bible of Dreams," saying, "I think that is publishable" (Kukil 481).

This story provides myriad avenues for essays and research papers. As with almost all of Plath's work, there is an undeniable note of autobiography. But, as has been discussed throughout the book, to read anything by Plath as mere recording of her personal feelings and the events of her life is to miss many great options about which you can write. As is the case in *The Bell Jar*, this story features a first-person narrator who lets readers in on her thoughts. She sees the troubles people go through and believes they all come down to one thing: panic. The name she has assigned to the root of the chaos is Johnny Panic. The narrator uses her position to fulfill her goal of becoming a "dream connoisseur," a collector of other people's dreams (Plath 158). She is not interested in sharing these dreams or using them against the people who dream them; instead, she calls herself a "lover of dreams for Johnny Panic's sake, the Maker of them all" (157). In this passage readers can determine some of her views on psychotherapy:

> Now the routine in our office is very different from the routine in Skin Clinic, for example, or in Tumor. The other clinics have strong similarities to each other; none are like ours. In our clinic, treatment doesn't get prescribed. It is invisible. It goes right on in those little cubicles, each with its desk, its two chairs, its window and its door with the opaque glass rectangle set in wood. There is a certain spiritual purity about this kind of doctoring. I can't help feeling the special privilege of my position as Assistant Secretary in the Adult Psychiatric Clinic. My sense of pride is borne out by the rude invasions of other clinics into our cubicles on certain days of the week for lack of space elsewhere: our building is a very old one, and the facilities have not expanded with the expanding needs of time. On these days of overlap the contrast between us and the other clinics is marked. (Plath 159)

The narrator sees psychiatry as removed from other areas of medicine, made plain by her emphasis on the similarity of the other clinics compared to hers. She takes pride in the work she does at the clinic, but not because of the duties; she seems more proud of belonging to an entity that does not fit with the norm. What does that say about the narrator? What ideas can readers get about Plath's own views on psychotherapy, especially knowing that she underwent a variety of therapies after she attempted suicide? As you reread this passage, note how she describes the treatment as "invisible," meaning talk therapy does not offer the comforting tangibles like surgery or medication. By describing the way the other specialties intrude on the clinic's space on busy days, she is also hinting that these other areas of medicine trample over psychotherapy and crowd it out, suggesting it is not seen as valuable or necessary compared to those other fields.

Another point to note here is the narrator's feeling that there is "a certain spiritual purity" in the treatment offered by her clinic. What is it that the narrator sees as making it spiritual? Why does she call the book she wants to fill with peoples' dreams a Bible? The narrator suggests medicine, and in this case especially psychoanalysis, is afforded a stature usually reserved for religion. Later in the story she describes someone who "lives in holy worship of Johnny Panic," furthering the comparison between medicine and religion.

TOPICS AND STRATEGIES

The ideas presented in this section are meant not as blueprints for you to use for your essay but instead as triggers for your own ideas and analyses of "Johnny Panic and the Bible of Dreams." As you think about how to proceed with your own paper or essay, carefully consider your own reactions to and thoughts about the story. Decide why it is something, a turn of phrase or maybe an image or a reference, caught your eye or made you think. Think of the suggestions below as tools to help you put into words those reactions you had.

Themes

Since Plath herself received outpatient therapy for depression, it is almost certain that she was referencing some of that experience when she wrote this story. Using that as a topic for an essay or research project undoubtedly offers a wide array of possible avenues for you to pursue as you write your paper. However, it is important to remember that there are other themes in the story that may not seem as obvious but also offer very rich possibilities for papers. Some of the themes are familiar from other of Plath's works, but that does not mean that they are treated the same in those works; as you decide on a theme about which to write, think about how Plath uses the genre of the short story to express her thoughts about the theme or themes you choose.

Sample Topics:

1. **Psychotherapy and other treatments for mental illness:**
   What does a person gain when he or she is treated by psychotherapy? What does one lose in this treatment?

   In letters she wrote to her benefactor, Olive Higgins Prouty,
   Plath indicated she was troubled by the treatment she received
   in 1953 after her suicide attempt, including some concern about
   the doctor who treated her; according to Jacqueline Rose, who
   writes extensively about Plath's treatment for mental illness,
   Plath's doctor even considered paying for her continuing treatment "because she was such an interesting case" (83). Does this
   idea of the patient as a "case" manifest itself in the story? What
   might Plath be saying about a trade-off a person makes when
   he or she has psychiatric therapy? What statements might she
   be making about the treatment being worse than the ailment?
   Do you see Plath saying anything positive about the treatment
   being offered in the clinic in which the narrator works?

2. **Religion:** Is Plath making a statement about religion in this
   story? If so, what is she saying?

   In January 1959, Plath writes in her journal, "Am reading the
   book of Job: great peace derived therefrom. Shall read the
   Bible: symbolic meaning, even though the belief in a moral
   God-structured universe not there" (Kukil 462). Where do you
   see this dichotomy of belief and doubt in this story? Does the
   narrator actually achieve peace at the end of the story? Consider the settings in which the narrator makes her comments
   about religion; what is the significance of the placement of
   these religious references in a place where people are treated
   for mental illness? If you do not think Plath is making a statement about religion, why all the religious imagery?

3. **The environment:** Where does Plath point out the environmental dangers of modern society?

Tracy Brain argues that this story "explores the physical and mental damage sustained by the individuals who live in the toxic, mechanized mid-twentieth century of the cold war" with "an environmental context—a concern with individuals and their connections to their world—that moves beyond any representation of events from Plath's 'real' life" (Brain 93). Brain also believes Plath makes careful choices when writing about the other clinics that intrude on the narrator's; they "deal with illnesses which are often the result of environmental damage" (96). Where do you see Plath making these statements? What does she point to as the results of this pollution and environmental damage? How do the dreams of the patients reflect a concern for such things? How does that relate to the experience the narrator has in the clinic?

4. **Dreams and reality:** What is the relation between dreams and reality in this story? Are dreams a reflection of reality or an escape from it?

In the story, the narrator connects patients to their dreams: "As far as I'm concerned, the dreams single them out more than any Christian name" (Plath 157). What does that mean? How is it borne out in what the narrator says in the story? She also connects the patients' dreams to what they do for a living. Why do you think she makes those connections? What is Plath, especially via the narrator, suggesting peoples' dreams say about them? Are dreams an accurate reflection of the dreamer? The narrator seems to think so, but is she accurate or reliable in that assertion? Dreams and reality in this story can become hard to discern. Do people create or control their own dreams and thus their own reality? The narrator in the story hides the fact that she is reading and writing about all these dreams. Is Plath suggesting people should hide their dreams? Do they betray the dreamers? Did the narrator's betray her?

Characters

The characters in this story play an integral role in helping tell the narrator's story. Although they all seem concerned for the narrator, by the end of the story readers are left to wonder whether those characters are actually evil or if they are actually helping the narrator. The narrator's disjointed telling of the story makes her seem troubled, yet most readers will find it extremely difficult not to root for her and sympathize with the plight she finds herself in at the end of the story.

Perhaps the only one in the story truly able to help the narrator, at least in her view, is Johnny Panic himself. Johnny Panic is key to this story, but can he actually be considered a character? Based on what you know about Plath and her own experience with depression and her attempted suicide, do you think she would have known Johnny Panic? As you reread the story, think about how the narrator portrays each character in the story as dependent on Johnny Panic in some way. What name might the other characters give to Johnny Panic?

Sample Topics:

1. **Miss Taylor** What is Miss Taylor's role in the story?

   How does Miss Taylor either support or negate the narrator's views on dreams and panic? Her career at the clinic was born the same year the narrator was born, which the narrator considers important enough to note. The narrator also notes that "if the building caught fire" she would risk her own life to save the books of statistics (Plath 163); what is the significance of that obsession? How does that coincide with the narrator's obsession for the records of patients' dreams? Why, then, is the narrator so worried about Miss Taylor catching her reading the records of patient dreams? Does she play a role in what happens to the narrator at the end of the story, either purposefully or inadvertently?

2. **The narrator:** Why is she so fascinated by other peoples' dreams that she is driven to create and even worship Johnny Panic?

   The narrator concocts Johnny Panic as the great Dream Maker, the driving force behind all the dreams she hears about and reads about. Why does the narrator feel the need to name this panic? Is the narrator in this story reliable—can readers take her seriously? Could she be dreaming the whole thing? Although there are notes of Plath's own life in this story, there are also notable differences (the narrator is 33, but when the story was written, Plath would have been in her twenties; the narrator is presumably single, but at the time Plath wrote this story, she was married to Ted Hughes). How could you argue that Plath did not intend for the narrator to be a mere replica of herself? Does Johnny Panic really save her at the end of the story? What does it mean that she is talking in the past tense throughout the story?

3. **The clinic director:** Why is he the one to send the narrator to her ultimate fate?

He is not physically present in a lot of the action that takes place, yet his presence is a constant undercurrent throughout the story. How does that sort of presence illustrate his power in the clinic? When the director first finds the narrator reading the old dream records, he seems kindly, even gentle toward her. What does he mean when he says to her, "Why, we need you more than you know"? (169). Has he been planning this treatment for the narrator for a long time? Do you think he colluded with Miss Milleravage to do this to the narrator? He is the only man, besides Johnny Panic, with a major role in the story—how is that significant?

4. **Miss Milleravage:** She is not a doctor or a nurse, so why is she the one who is preparing the narrator for the treatment at the end of the story?

The narrator is not unfamiliar with Miss Milleravage—she has seen her before: "Something about her merely smoking and drinking her coffee in the cafeteria at the ten o'clock break put me off so I never went to sit next to her again" (Plath 162). Even her name, which includes the word *ravage*, suggests her bent toward violence. Does Miss Milleravage worship the "five false priests" who take over once she has prepared the narrator for the electrotherapy, or is she acting on her own behalf? How do the narrator's descriptions of Miss Milleravage emphasize how frightening she can be? Why does she say about the narrator, "My baby, my own baby's come back to me" (Plath 171)? What does the narrator mean when she says, "The machine betrays them [Miss Milleravage and the clinic director]" (Plath 172)?

History and Context

In one of the appendices for *The Unabridged Journals,* Kukil includes numerous examples of Plath's writings about the patients she saw come through the clinic at Massachusetts General (Kukil 624); some of those obviously served as inspiration for the dreams in this story. Plath's own experiences as a patient in a clinic as well as working in one had an undeniable impact on her, which is reflected in this story.

Plath's experiences were likely influenced by major changes going on in psychotherapy and other treatments for mental illness in the 1950s. Mental health treatment, including psychoanalysis, psychiatry, and dream analysis, was undergoing many changes. The aftermath of World War II was a driving factor in the growth of psychotherapy in its various forms, as well as a source of great disturbance for Plath herself. As in other of her works, current events play an important role in the story of Johnny Panic:

> The narrator's interest in making a book of the dreams of the patients suggests the way in which Plath uses history and views herself in relation to it. The landscape of her late work is a contemporary social landscape. It goes back in time to encompass ... significant historical events ... and ... is perhaps obsessed with, the major historical event of her time, the Second World War. (Annas 110)

As you decide on a topic, consider the current events of Plath's time and think about how they are reflected in the story.

Sample Topics:

1. **World War II and its aftermath, including the cold war:** How have the patients, as well as the main characters in the story, been damaged by World War II and the ensuing cold war?

Langdon Hammer writes about Plath's reactions to war, noting, "War inspired in her horror, dread, outrage, disgust. It also inspired curiosity: she wanted to know what war is like" (147). Miss Milleravage mentions her work in London and a friend she tried to look up after the war. She seems unmoved that her friend "must've gone down . . . in the bombings" (Plath 163). How is a postwar ethos communicated in this story? Does Plath present an apocalyptic view of society through her description of people's dreams and the final treatment she undergoes? Can the narrator in the story be seen as a sort of spy? How is her recording of the dreams of others dangerous for the other side? Who exactly *is* the other side?

2. **Roles of women:** What do the actions taken by the women in this story say about women's roles in general?

Miss Taylor is extremely dedicated to her job at the clinic. Miss Milleravage is the one who is administering the final punishment (as the narrator sees it) to the narrator. Yet the men in the story (the clinic director and Johnny Panic) are the ones who presumably hold all the power. Is Plath arguing that women actually have more power? Would things have been different if one of the women in the story had been the clinic director? How so? Would the narrator's fate have been any different? Miss Milleravage is not technically qualified to administer the electrotherapy to the narrator; why is she the one to do it rather than the clinic director?

3. **Privacy:** What happens to people when their private thoughts are made public?

What is Plath saying about privacy in this story? Do the dreamers give up ownership of their innermost thoughts when they talk to a therapist? Since the narrator is continually trying to sneak into patient records, the notion of privacy runs throughout this work. The narrator suggests that in private (including in our dreams) we are someone else, confiding in readers, "In the privacy of my one-room apartment I call

myself secretary to none other than Johnny Panic himself"
(Plath 156). Brain believes in this story Plath is pointing out
that "no boundary is impermeable" and that the intrusions by
the other clinics show "nobody, and no thing, whether positively or negatively charged, human comfort or poison, can be
held off as separate" (96). Why does the narrator keep her goal
(creating the Bible of Dreams) a secret? Does she believe she is
invading patients' privacy by reading and writing about their
dreams, or does she think she is doing them a great service?

Philosophy and Ideas

Although dreams are the most notable subject in this story, writing figures prominently throughout the work; the narrator is reading about
the patients and their dreams with the ultimate goal of writing down
what she reads and amassing all of the stories into one book, the Bible of
Dreams. Yet the narrator's obsession with writing this volume gets her in
trouble and presumably deems her mentally unstable enough to warrant
electrotherapy. The way that Plath equates the therapy with punishment
and even death is significant; she brings into question the limits of psychotherapy as well as the attitudes people have about it. Note, though,
that there are no doctors who feature prominently here; instead, the
main characters are members of the nonmedical staff. It is significant
to note that the therapy-cum-punishment she receives at the end of the
story is "prescribed" by the clinic director and administered by his secretary; presumably no doctor is present or involved in the decision. What
might Plath be saying about the business of medicine rather than the
practice of it?

Sample Topics:

1. **Fitting in:** Why are the patients in this story so worried about
   what is in their dreams? What do they have to fear if they do
   not fit in?

   Does the belief that it is important to fit in and reflect the
   standards and beliefs of mainstream society make people too
   quick to judge whether someone needs to be put away or, in
   this case, to decide what treatment they need? The narrator

in this story gets caught doing something seemingly innocent, yet she is, at least in her estimation, punished for her
acts by electrotherapy. The dreamers in the story seek therapy because they fear being seen as odd or what their dreams
might say about them. Is it because what is going on in their
unconscious makes them fear they are capable of something
awful? Is this why the narrator is so careful to hide her interest in the dreams, because she knows her devotion to Johnny
Panic will signal to people that she is not normal or that she is
not trying to fit in with the system at the clinic?

2. **Writing:** What does the narrator hope to accomplish by writing
   the Bible of Dreams? Why not find out about the dreams from
   Johnny Panic himself?

   The story's narrator is more interested in the written accounts
   of the dreams than in listening to people talk about them.
   Why? She reads through records that have already been committed to paper; why is it necessary to rewrite them for the
   Bible of Dreams? Is she merely copying what has already been
   written about the dreams, or do you think she is actually add-
   ing to them? One biographer argues Plath is addressing "an
   issue which has ramifications which go beyond the personal
   drama played out by the protagonists to touch on the most
   fundamental aspects of the way our culture institutionally
   encodes the relationship between language and psychic life"
   (Rose 83). Is there a message here that once a person's dreams
   (or feelings or beliefs) are committed to paper, they can be
   used against the dreamer? Is writing for the narrator cathartic
   in some way?

3. **Medicine as a business:** What is the goal of the Adult Psychiatric Clinic, according to the narrator? Why would she try to
   sabotage the doctors and staff in their pursuit of that goal?

   The narrator despairs at how the doctors are curing patients
   and sending them out into the world, robbing her of material

for the Bible of Dreams and noting she has to work faster "if only to counteract those doctors" (Plath 166). What does she lose, or what does she think Johnny Panic loses, if the patients are cured too quickly? Critic Tracy Brain argues the narrator does not want to help the doctors and psychiatrists make their money ("dream-gathering for worldly ends: health and money, money and health"); since she does not follow the rules of the consumer culture in which she operates, she must be punished (97). How is medicine, especially psychiatry, portrayed here as part of the consumer culture? Aside from the fees charged, how does the clinic profit from curing patients quickly? Why would the narrator be disturbed by that?

Form and Genre

Linda Wagner-Martin lauds this story, saying, "It was a breakthrough in fiction to a recognizable artistic voice that Sylvia had not yet made in her poetry" (*Biography* 155–56). Yet when the American version of the collection of stories titled *Johnny Panic and the Bible of Dreams* was published in Great Britain in 1979, "no news items or reviews of the book appeared at all" (Alexander 354). Many critics argue that poetry was the only genre Plath really excelled at and that the short stories she wrote are barely worthy of publication.

Even Plath herself seemed to harbor some mixed feelings about the short story; on one hand, she writes in her journal that "Johnny Panic" was one of the few stories she could reread and that she thought was quite good (Kukil 515). On the other hand, she also expressed some dissatisfaction with her short stories in general and this one specifically: "If only I could break through in one story. Johnny Panic too much a fantasy. If only I could get it real" (Kukil 509). As you reread the story and think about what to write about it, consider how you think Plath's work here compares to her work in poetry. How does reading "Johnny Panic and the Bible of Dreams" help you think about her work as a whole? Do you see this as a jumping-off point for some of the poetry she would write later in her career? Which genre do you think is best suited for Plath's messages? How might you categorize her writing style based on this story? Would it be different than in the other genres she uses?

Sample Topics:

1. **Language and sentence structure:** How does the structure of this short story mimic the feel of a dream?

   As you reread the story, consider how Plath controls the pace of the story and how she uses language and structure to create a specific tone for the piece. This is an early work for her, written before much of the poetry that would make her famous. As one writer notes of this story, the "movement from long run-on paragraphing to single lines with underscore emotion shows her developing skill" and the use of sentence fragments to highlight emotion are purposeful moves on Plath's part (Wagner-Martin, *Plath* 57). How do these tactics relate and/ or compare to her poetry? Do you see similar tactics being used in Plath's other works? Plath was a stickler for reading her poetry out loud; how does this story sound when you read it out loud compared to reading it silently?

2. **Voice:** How does the voice of the narrator in "Johnny Panic and the Bible of Dreams" compare to the voices of the speakers in Plath's poetry?

   How does Plath use the genre of the short story to communicate her views, concerns, and ideas differently than in poetry or her novel? Many readers cannot help but see the voice in Plath's work as her own, but it is important to understand that she was not merely recapping her own experiences; she created characters with their own voices. How would you characterize the narrator's voice in this work? Is she angry? Is the narrator actually, as she argues, the only one who really understands what is going on at the clinic? Wagner-Martin characterizes the voice of the narrator as "natural-sounding . . . a slangy, tough woman's voice" (*Biography* 156) with a lot of power. How is her voice unique from Plath's, meaning how is her story not the same as Plath's? How would you describe the voice Plath uses in her writing? Or would you argue that she uses multiple voices? How does the incorporation of dialogue at the end of the story help to reinforce or weaken the voice of the narrator?

3. **Satire and humor:** How can this story be read as humorous? What or who is Plath satirizing in this story?

Probably largely because of Plath's history, not many readers think of Plath's work as humorous, yet she includes satire in her work and sometimes treats major issues with some humor. Wagner-Martin sees the writing in this story as "humorous prose" (*Biography* 155). Part of the humor comes in her descriptions of the people she works with, especially Miss Milleravage. The narrator's descriptions of the dreams she hears and reads about are not sympathetic or respectful; rather, they sound more like gossipy interpretations. What does her rather nonchalant treatment of the analysis of these dreams communicate? What does it mean that the narrator is speaking in the past tense throughout the story, almost as if in a therapy session? What might Plath be saying about the field of dream analysis as a whole? Is she poking fun at herself anywhere here?

Language, Symbols, and Imagery

Electrotherapy is a key element in "Johnny Panic and the Bible of Dreams," as well as in other works by Plath, specifically *The Bell Jar.* Jacqueline Rose argues Plath is making a statement that "the damage of electrotherapy is not just what it does *to* the speaker, something negative it forces upon her, but equally what it takes *away*—a negativity which she identifies no less firmly as something internal to herself" (Rose 57). References to religion are obviously another major element in this story; what effect does that have on readers when those familiar religious references are paired with powerful images of what seems like an electrocution?

Through the combination of these two elements, Plath creates a surreal scene at the end of the book that brings up a range of questions for readers about what might actually be happening to the narrator. Her own background with the Unitarian Church likely plays a role in this;

she struggled with issues of religion and belief at times in her own life. As you think about a writing project related to this story, consider how the entire story leads readers to the dramatic final scene with the narrator and Miss Milleravage and the appearance of Johnny Panic. What significant images along the way hint at or even prepare the reader for the final scene?

Sample Topics:

1. **Religion and the church:** Why does the narrator connect what goes on in the clinic where she works with church? Is she arguing that psychotherapy is like a religious experience?

   How is what the narrator experiences at the end of the story like a religious experience? She makes references to the "wafer of forgetfulness" and "the crown of wire" (Plath 171), and Johnny Panic, the god of the dream world, appears to her because "He forgets not his own" (172). Why does Plath incorporate the specific religious images and references she does? What does all the religious imagery mean? Plath had some concerns about her own psychiatric treatment. What is she saying about the connection between medicine and religion? How does the narrator illustrate this point? How does her experience complicate what you know about Plath's experiences? Is Plath suggesting that medicine is afforded too high a status—that people have faith in medicine as they do in religion? What is the significance of the religious references becoming more prominent as the story progresses?

2. **Authority and power:** Who has actual power and authority in this story?

   There are several characters featured prominently in this story, yet none of them are doctors, the only ones qualified to treat patients. There are "five false priests" who come to the room at the end of the story to help administer the treatment (Plath 171). In the eyes of the narrator, Johnny Panic is the one who is really running the show. Is he the ultimate authority for the narrator, or is it the clinic director? Or Miss Milleravage? Or even Miss Taylor? The narrator sees that any of the three of them could ruin her plan to create the Bible of Dreams for Johnny Panic. Think about what Plath is saying about the control people have over their own thoughts and actions. When it comes to dreams, is the dreamer in charge? Or do the dreamers have no control or not want control because they want to know what is wrong with them (or think there is something wrong with them) because of their dreams? Do you give up authority when you confide your deepest thoughts to someone else, specifically a doctor? Think about Plath's own experiences with her treatment for depression and decide how those experiences might have shaped the portrayal of authority figures in this story.

3. **Johnny Panic:** What is he symbolic of? Why does the narrator worship him?

   Johnny Panic is not a real person, yet he is a crucial character in the story. How would you put into words what he symbolizes? Plath does not explicitly define his presence and function, yet she offers hints throughout the story. The narrator refers to Johnny Panic as a god and talks about worshiping him, so there are some seemingly obvious religious overtones. Why does the narrator worship Johnny Panic? What does he give her that she cannot get elsewhere? Why has she created him? Does his existence reinforce the idea that she is insane, or could it actually illustrate her sanity? Why is the clinic so intent on eliminating Johnny Panic? The machine the narrator is hooked to at the end of the story is "the latest model in Johnny-Panic-Killers" and the priests' "one lifework is to unseat Johnny Panic from his own throne" (Plath 171); what will be gained if Johnny Panic is eliminated? Is the entire story of Johnny Panic merely a dream the narrator is having?

4. **Light and lighting:** Why do light and lighting play such an important role in the narrator's telling of the story?

Throughout the story the narrator makes reference to lighting and sources of light. What is the significance of those references? In one instance she discusses how she had the setting of a dream lit, noting "I had the whole scene lighted . . . not with candles, but with the ice-bright fluorescence that makes skin look green" (Plath 161); when she decides to stay overnight at the clinic to read dream files she avoids turning on the overhead light, choosing a "sallow twenty-five-watt affair" (167); and white light is a major element in the final scene of the book. Why is the narrator, and thus Plath, so careful to get the lighting right in this story? What do the various types of light signify? Does light illuminate the truth? Does it uncover people? Is light a positive force or a negative force in this story?

Compare and Contrast Essays

Since Plath wrote in three genres, the poem, the short story, and the novel, comparing and contrasting her works for an essay can be a fruitful venture. Because there is so much material available to readers that Plath herself never intended to be published, some readers and critics have reservations about comparing what might be lesser-developed stories to the works Plath intended to publish. Margaret Atwood voiced this concern when she wrote, "'What writer of sane mind would willingly give to the world her undergraduate short stories, her disgruntled jottings on the doings of unpleasant neighbors, her embarrassing attempts to write formula magazine fiction?'" (qtd. in Alexander 354). If Plath did not mean for something to be read by others, comparing it to something that she wished to publish may not be a wise choice.

As you consider which works to use for a compare and contrast project, think about what you want to say about the pieces you are thinking of using. Do you see similar themes? How are they developed in each of the stories? Are there common images? Do you see one piece as a springboard to the other? Like other artists and writers, Plath's work is often categorized by when she wrote it, or where she was living, or when it was published (some posthumously), so doing some research to get the particulars of the piece will be helpful as you begin to write.

Sample Topics:

1. *The Bell Jar:* How do you see "Johnny Panic and the Bible of Dreams" as a step toward *The Bell Jar*?

   Thinking especially about the final pages of the short story, where the narrator is being prepared for electrotherapy, consider how her experience is similar to Esther Greenwood's. Compare and contrast the images of electroshock therapy in each of the works. Does either of the young women think she needs the therapy? Are readers led to believe they need the therapy? How do the experiences leading up to the therapy differ for each of the women? Where do you see similar language used to describe the experiences of each of the young women? In *The Bell Jar*, Esther's dreams, especially about the fig tree, play an important role in her life. How would the narrator in "Johnny Panic" view Esther's dreams? How do dreams affect each of the young women? Both of the narrators speak of what happened as if it is in the past; what does that mean about the treatment's success or not? Does reading both of the works help you draw some conclusions about Plath's feelings about her own treatment for depression?

2. **D.H. Lawrence's "The Woman Who Rode Away":** How can "Johnny Panic and the Bible of Dreams" be seen as a response to or even rebuttal of the D.H. Lawrence story?

   Feminist critic Sandra Gilbert sees "Johnny Panic and the Bible of Dreams" as a rewrite of Lawrence's "The Woman Who Rode Away," noting the common elements of "a thirty-three-year-old misbehaving woman . . . the five robed priests, the sacrifice and ritual that accompanies it" and sees Plath as creating "a true intertextual answer" to Lawrence and "whatever misogynists existed in her writing life" (Wagner-Martin, *Literary Life* 58–59). What is being said about women and women's roles in Lawrence's story? How does Plath respond to those statements in "Johnny Panic"? Can you find any other evidence that Plath read the Lawrence work?

3. **"Poem for a Birthday:"** How does Plath address issues of nature and rebirth in each of these works?

"Poem for a Birthday" features more overt references to nature than "Johnny Panic and the Bible of Dreams," yet there are some strong arguments to be made that Plath is making significant statements about nature and the environment in this story. Brain argues that the connection between this short story and the poem is clear and "the link between the two texts . . . concerns nature, and the individual's access to it" (94). What is Plath saying inhibits the individual's ability to access nature? Also, as you reread each of the works, look for a story embedded in a story; in the poem, there are poems situated within a poem. In the short story, dreams are situated within dreams. How does that sort of telescoping narrative influence how readers see the story being told?

Bibliography and Online Resources for "Johnny Panic and the Bible of Dreams"

Alexander, Paul. *Rough Magic: A Biography of Sylvia Plath.* New York: DeCapo, 1999. Print.

Annas, Pamela J. *A Disturbance in Mirrors: The Poetry of Sylvia Plath.* New York: Greenwood P, 1988. Print.

Brain, Tracy. *The Other Sylvia Plath.* Harlow, England: Pearson, 2001. Print.

Hammer, Langdon. "Plath at War." *Eye Rhymes: Sylvia Plath's Art of the Visual.* Kathleen Connors and Sally Bayley, Eds. Oxford: Oxford U P, 2007. 145–157. Print.

Kukil, Karen V., Ed. *The Unabridged Journals of Sylvia Plath.* New York: Anchor Books, 2000. Print.

Plath, Sylvia. "Johnny Panic and the Bible of Dreams." *Johnny Panic and the Bible of Dreams.* New York: Harper, 2000. 156–72. Print.

Rose, Jacqueline. *The Haunting of Sylvia Plath.* Cambridge, MA: Harvard U P, 1992. Print.

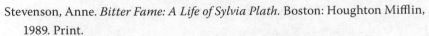
Stevenson, Anne. *Bitter Fame: A Life of Sylvia Plath.* Boston: Houghton Mifflin, 1989. Print.

Wagner-Martin, Linda. *Sylvia Plath: A Biography.* New York: Simon and Schuster, 1987. Print.

———. *Sylvia Plath: A Literary Life.* Hampshire, England: Macmillan P, 1999. Print.

"THE COLOSSUS"

READING TO WRITE

"The Colossus" was part of a collection of the same name, published in England in 1960 and then in the United States two years later. Although she had had numerous works that appeared in magazines and other venues, *The Colossus and Other Poems* was Plath's first collection to be published. When she got the good news that Alfred A. Knopf publishers had bought the book for publication in the United States, but they had decided to cut ten of the poems in the British version, Sylvia was excited nonetheless and was "willing to do whatever Knopf requested" to see the book published in the States (Wagner-Martin, *Biography* 184). Plath did ask to have some of the poems Knopf wanted removed put back in because, as she noted, "the collection had a theme, the person who is 'broken and mended,' beginning with the smashed colossus and ending with the self" (Wagner-Martin, *Biography* 184). In her journals she expresses fear that the collection would never be published in the United States, which likely explains why she was so happy to let Knopf make changes to the collection.

This poem was one of several Plath wrote when she and her husband resided at a writers colony called Yaddo in 1959. The colony was in Saratoga Springs, New York, and her experience there proved to be an important one for her as a poet. "The Colossus" was written there, as were other poems in the collection; she practiced her craft at the colony, along with meditation and hypnotism exercises that she believed heightened her creativity; "that the book carried as its title one of the Yaddo poems, and that it concluded with . . . one of the last things Sylvia wrote at Yaddo" (Wagner-Martin, *Biography* 168) demonstrated that her fall experience at the writers colony was crucial to her development as a poet.

That development is clear in the purposeful way Plath approaches language and images in this poem. Many readers think of Plath's work as so autobiographical that they fail to see the writerly tactics she employs in her poetry as well as in her prose. Linda Wagner-Martin notes that this collection showed Plath's effort to be more informal in her language "as a way to get rid of what she called 'drawing room' speech. She wanted a voice that was witty, wry, American, brazen, arrogant and, at times, comic—like those of Welty, Roth, and Salinger" (*Biography* 165). Plath herself writes in her journal that she finds this poem "colorful and amusing" (Kukil 523), further demonstrating that her writing was not, as many are quick to believe, merely the depressed outpourings of a suicidal woman.

Of course, when reading this poem it is important to consider that Plath lost her father when she was very young and that she mourned that loss her entire life:

> The poem 'The Colossus' is apparently about Sylvia's father, pictured as the ruin of a huge statue, over which the daughter crawls as she tries to repair it. The poem draws on imagery she had often used. . . . It describes Ouija board sessions in which her father was called 'colossus' or 'Prince Otto,' as well as Sylvia's impression of the Elgin marbles and the many Egyptian colossi in the British Museum. Her tone of wry chagrin is clear from the start. (Wagner-Martin, *Biography* 166)

Reading "The Colossus" in this light can be especially useful when you think about writing an essay about the poem. Finding a balance between reading Plath's work as strictly autobiographical and as carefully crafted art is important as you decide on a topic. Obviously her personal experience played a role in her work, but she also made distinct decisions about creating a piece of poetry that was not necessarily just a reflection of her life. Plath is considered a prominent figure in the confessional poetry movement; confessional poetry is defined as "the poetry of the personal" that often explores "[p]rivate experiences with and feelings about death, trauma, depression and relationships . . . often in an autobiographical manner" ("A Brief Guide").

Important to remember, however, is that "[t]he confessional poets were not merely recording their emotions on paper; craft and construction were extremely important to their work" ("A Brief Guide"). As you read "The Colossus," look for that attention to construction along with the more personal content of the piece. Both of these elements, personal experience and craft, are apparent in the first two stanzas of the poem:

> I shall never get you put together entirely.
> Pieced, glued, and properly jointed.
> Mule-bray, pig-grunt and bawdy cackles
> Proceed from your great lips.
> It's worse than a barnyard.
>
> Perhaps you consider yourself an oracle,
> Mouthpiece of the dead, or of some god or other.
> Thirty years now I have labored
> To dredge the silt from your throat.
> I am none the wiser. (Plath 1–10)

The first and last lines of this section especially point to the confessional nature of this poem, as the speaker in the poem addresses the subject of the poem and expresses her inability to piece together a relationship with him. When you read these stanzas, you can see how Plath is writing about the speaker's attempt to reassemble someone from whom she wishes to gain something—in this case, knowledge. The speaker realizes she is not having success at her endeavor because not only is she unable to put the pieces together correctly, but also she cannot understand the utterances (brays, grunts, and cackles) the improperly put together colossus is sharing. And, as the speaker says, even after 30 years of trying to clear away the silt, she still has not gained any of the knowledge for which she is looking.

Linda Wagner-Martin notes this quest in her biography of Plath; "As the poet mends the statue, she regards it as an oracle, the source of wisdom she desperately needs but cannot quite understand" (166). This statement also hints at myriad possible topics for an essay about this poem. There are references made to personal experience, but there are also many opportunities to explore allusions to mythology, images of nature, and even commentary on societal norms that reflect a value of patriarchal power.

TOPICS AND STRATEGIES

As you read through the following ideas for essays, do remember that they are just that—ideas. Your own reading of the poem may yield variations on these suggested topics or you may find an avenue not mentioned here that you wish to pursue. As you think about how to start your paper or essay, think about your own reactions to the poem. What stands out to you? Are there words you don't know or references you don't quite understand? Sometimes one of your best resources for a project can be a dictionary or an encyclopedia. In the following sections, some of the references and terms will be discussed, but don't hesitate to find out more about them or to look up information for clarification. Having a complete grasp on the individual words in a poem is an important first step in getting prepared to write about that poem.

Themes

One thing that is commonly discussed in regard to this poem (as well as in other of Plath's works, like "Daddy") is the allusion to the ancient Greek figure Electra. Electra is a character in the story of Agamemnon, first recorded in the *Oresteia* by the Greek poet Aeschylus. Agamemnon, a powerful king, returns from the Trojan War and is killed by his wife, Clytemnestra, who is having an affair with Agamemnon's cousin. Their daughter, Electra (along with her brother, Orestes), vows to find out who killed her father and avenge his death. The story has been retold over the centuries; depending on which version of the story you read, either Orestes or he and his sister, Electra, kill their mother because she murdered their father.

Based on Plath's journal entries, it is not hard to see how Plath's feelings translate into a version of this myth. She writes in one entry that she feels her mother killed her father by "marrying him too old, by marrying him sick to death and dying, by burying him every day since in her heart, mind, and words" (Kukil 431). Lynda Bundtzen, a Plath biographer, notes that, like Electra, Plath was "compelled by blood-guilt and revenge to persist in her work" (188), much of which reflects her feelings about the loss of her father.

Sample Topics:

1. **The Electra complex:** How do you see Plath, both as herself and as the speaker in the poem, playing the role of Electra in "The

Colossus"? What specific words, images, and phrases support your point?

At least one critic argues that "Plath is acutely aware of her supposed Electra complex" and that even her suicide is "an act of love and longing for a union with a dead father who has, in her imagination at least, become a god, a colossus" (Bundtzen 134). Based on your reading of this poem, what do you think the speaker hopes to obtain from her reassembled father? How do you see the idea of vengeance for his death reflected in the poem? In line 16 the speaker sees "A blue sky out of the Oresteia"; does the context of that reference fit with your understanding of the story of Electra? How has Plath personalized the story in this poem?

2. **Guilt:** Does the speaker seem to feel any responsibility for the death of her father? Or is her guilt based on her inability to piece the colossus together properly?

   Wagner-Martin believes "Plath's writing often focuses on the guilt the daughter feels for her bereavement—she has somehow been responsible for [her father's] death" (*Literary Life* 12). How do you see that manifested in this poem? How will putting him back together again help her overcome those feelings of guilt? How does any guilt she feels work with or against a desire for vengeance (think of the story of Electra)? Can you read this poem as the daughter telling the father *he* should feel guilt for leaving her? Could you argue that the speaker/daughter actually feels guilty because she is not bereaved enough by the loss of her father?

3. **Masculine influence:** How does the speaker in this poem allude to the effects the loss of the masculine influence of the colossus/father has had on her?

   In her journal, Plath writes that "a central metaphor for my childhood, my poems, and my artists' subconscious" is seen in "the father image—relating to my own father, the buried male muse & god-creator risen to by my mate in Ted" (Kukil 381). Where do you see the father figure as muse in this poem? How does the colossus inspire her? How do you see the speaker making a connection between the image of the father and her future relationships with men? Where in the poem do you see the speaker as specifically addressing the masculine elements of the colossus she is trying to piece together? What is it about those elements that seems especially important to the speaker? Why?

4. **Layers of one's past:** How is this poem a reflection of Plath working through her own past? How does the confessional genre of poetry work particularly well for this sort of exploration?

With her husband, Ted Hughes, Plath became interested in hypnotism; they used it as an avenue for "[r]eaching remote layers of consciousness" (Wagner-Martin, *Biography* 65). If the speaker is sweeping away the layers that have buried the colossus, what will she find when she finally gets to the statue? What do you suppose is the truth trapped within those layers of consciousness? What might the implied size of the colossus ("the weedy acres of your brow" and the "immense skull plates" in lines 13–14) indicate about the importance of the colossus in the speaker's past? What do the final lines of the poem indicate about the speaker's decision about continuing her efforts at unearthing the colossus?

Characters

In this poem, as in most, the speaker or narrator is usually an easy character to pick out. It can also help to imagine who the speaker is—of course, you know it is Sylvia Plath since she wrote the poem, but aside from just thinking about the writer, you need to consider how the writer creates a voice in the poem. Knowing the personal background of the poet and reading what others have written about this poem can make it obvious that the speaker's father is a character in this poem. However, it is important to avoid limiting your ideas about character to just the two because that can limit your ability to write about the poem. There are many useful and legitimate reasons for thinking about the speaker and her father as Sylvia and Otto Plath, but it is also necessary to consider why the father is characterized as a colossus and why the speaker in the poem is trying to reassemble him as such.

Sample Topics:

1. **The speaker:** Why is it so important to the speaker that she put the colossus back together again? What do you think is preventing her from piecing the colossus together properly or entirely?

   In this poem, "the reader is deliberately made aware that the speaker is comparing herself to a Greek heroine tending an idol" (Kroll 54). What is the significance of this comparison? Kroll also argues that "the speaker's identity is defined primarily in relation to her father" (82) in this poem. Is the speaker's identity more influenced by who her father was or by his loss? How is the speaker's life still affected by the father/colossus? Kroll notes this poem shows a "historical pattern (surviving without him is a kind of death) which ultimately requires [the father's] exorcism" (Kroll 122). How might piecing him together help the daughter achieve this exorcism? What is the speaker saying about herself, even indirectly, in this poem? One critic notes "the daughter-in-mourning seems to mark herself as lacking [the father's] greatness. Her despairing self-abasement before the remains of a father who cannot be recovered . . . can be seen as . . . ritual of self-humiliation and parodic miniaturization which cuts her down to size" (Britzolakis 179). How does your reading of the poem either support or refute this?

2. **The speaker's father:** What kind of person was the speaker's father? What in the speaker's description makes you think this?

   What role does the father in this poem continue to play in the speaker's life? Britzolakis argues that the more the daughter in this poem tries to retrieve and reassemble her father, the more "it recedes into myth and literature, like the legendary Colossus of Rhodes, which disappeared without a trace and may never have existed" (178). Do you believe the speaker has an accurate idea of what her father was like, or has her perception of him and his personality been too influenced by his absence from her life? The daughter seeks shelter in the statue's ear; what is the significance of her looking for protection there? What might she be saying about his attention to her when he was alive?

3. **The colossus:** What is the significance of referring to the father as a colossus in this poem? How do the descriptions of him as a statue illustrate what he was like when he was alive?

By definition, a colossus is a statue, especially one of large stature. How does the figure of the colossus differ from that of her father? Although they are compared to each other, they can still be differentiated. Why would Plath make this comparison? How might the comparison to a colossus ennoble the father? Or, conversely, how might it help to point out where he is lacking in nobility? Linda Wagner-Martin argues that in this poem Plath captures a "sense of the father as an unattainable sphinx-like statue, and entity more foreboding than real" (*Literary Life* 12). What features of the colossus speak to this idea of mystery (the sphinx)? Do you think the speaker is actually doing a better job at piecing the colossus together than she thinks she is? Is it possible the colossus can never be put together properly?

History and Context

The collection *The Colossus* is often referred to as transitional, reflecting Plath's maturation as a person and as a writer. Edward Butscher writes that this collection is

a curious mid-point between the two phases of Sylvia Plath's poetic development. In terms of basic techniques and language, it belongs firmly to the first phase. . . . Psychologically, the poem is a reliable indicator of Sylvia's growing realization that her father's ghost would not stay buried. (236)

The poems making up the collection, including "The Colossus," were written early in her relationship with Ted Hughes and as she was experiencing the move from the United States to England with him. She was, in a sense, leaving one life and starting a new one—moving from being predominantly a daughter and student to being a wife and writer. As you read through the poem and think about possible topics for projects and essays, consider this transition and how you see it influencing the poem.

Sample Topics:

1. **Otto Plath:** Does the father/colossus in this poem seem deserving of the daughter's efforts to put him back together?

   Otto Plath was a professor at Boston University before he died; how do you think his profession serves to reinforce the line "Perhaps you consider yourself an oracle" (6) in this poem? His death was the result of untreated diabetes—one of the results of his illness was that one of his legs had to be amputated. Is it too literal to see this as part of the speaker's efforts to put the colossus back together? Could you argue that the speaker is trying to achieve some sort of healing through piecing the colossus back together, both for herself and for her father? What exactly is Plath saying about her relationship with her father in this poem? Look into Plath's biographical information; where do you see Sylvia Plath using this poem as a personal effort to talk about her feelings about her father?

2. **Plath's relationship with her mother:** Plath, by her own admission, was angry at her mother, even holding her responsible for his death. How are those feelings manifested in this poem?

   The reference to the *Oresteia* is significant; what does the poet mean when she writes "A blue sky out of the Oresteia / Arches above us" (16–17)? Are readers to see this as an indication of Plath's ideas about her mother's role in Otto Plath's death?

Where do you see Plath's relationship with her mother, Aurelia, being addressed in this poem? Could you argue that the speaker's efforts to dig up and piece together the colossus are not only a way to get to know her father but also to save him from the death she sees as caused by her mother?

3. **Marriage and motherhood:** Plath was expecting her first child, Frieda, when she wrote "The Colossus." How do you see her new status and wife and soon-to-be mother expressed in this poem?

Do you see this poem as an effort on Plath's part to come to grips with her feelings about her own father as she was on the verge of becoming a parent herself? Are there images in the poem that could be seen as references to pregnancy? Although delighted to have a daughter, Plath was fairly convinced she was having a son; how does rebuilding the colossus help her to present a strong figure to a son? Why is that important to Plath? What might she think this oracle could tell her child? What images in the poem suggest to you that Plath is looking for guidance in raising her own child?

Philosophy and Ideas

There is no doubt that the death of her father, Otto, when she was eight years old had an indelible effect on Sylvia Plath and her work. In December 1958, shortly before she produced "The Colossus," she writes, "Me, I never knew the love of a father, the love of a steady blood-related man after the age of eight" (Kukil 431). There were a lot of other things going on in her life as well, including her marriage to Ted Hughes and her move to England with him. At the time, Plath was writing the poems for *The Colossus,* she was heavily influenced by her husband, Ted Hughes, who was a more famous and accomplished poet than she was at the time.

Importantly, though, Plath was also thinking about political issues and issues related to the rights of women. These concerns, most commonly associated with the more famous *Ariel* collection, were also present in *The Colossus,* as Christine Britzolakis points out:

The discourse of classicism associated with the paternal effigy is shadowed by intimations of a forgotten or obscured violence; the colossus, after all, is both an architectural ruin and a dismembered body which the speaker desperately longs to reconstruct. (179)

Lynda Bundtzen agrees, writing that while "The Colossus" is "clearly confessional . . . [it] also illuminate[s] woman's psyche as it is shaped by a patriarchal culture" (186). As she was writing for this collection, these issues became especially important for her when she became a mother and had to balance the roles of artist/writer and wife/mother.

Sample Topics:

1. **Femininity and femaleness:** What is unique about a daughter, rather than a son, unearthing and attempting to reassemble the colossus that is her father? How does the fact that the speaker is a woman affect the telling of the story?

   Bundtzen argues that Plath writes about a "mindless automatism that fulfills some order imposed from without" and "a female society with tremendous energies kept under lock and key" by that order (186). How does that relate to the speaker/daughter trying to resurrect her father so he can speak to her? Does the daughter believe the knowledge she gains from her oracle father will help her gain entry into that order? Bundtzen goes on to say, "Even if the father could speak, it is implied that he would have nothing to say; and the daughter meanwhile wastes her energies in this obsessive activity directed at giving him life" (186). Why would he have nothing to say? Is the implication that he would not speak to her because she is a daughter and not a son?

2. **Dichotomy and opposites:** Where do you see duality in this poem? Where does it seem to be two sides of the same coin, and where does it look like opposites?

   There are many opposites that enter into this poem: male/female, dead/alive, buried/unearthed, and noisy/silent. What do you think Plath is trying to demonstrate by bringing these opposites into the poem? Lynda Bundtzen sees a change in the daughter's attitude and finds it puzzling: "this double perspective—devoted and critical—in 'The Colossus' is confusing" (187). What do you make of this "double perspective"? Another instance of a double perspective is derived from the reader's standpoint. Tracy Brain points out that the biographical information in the first American version of this collection says:

> Plath's 'work reflects both her New England heritage and the landscape of England where she now makes her home'. Here, the central thing about Plath's work is seen as geographical and cultural: the presence of two nationalities and two landscapes in her writing. This strand of Plath's thought is every bit as important and prevalent as her alleged obsession with depression and death, yet national identity has all but vanished as a theme which might help us to understand her work. (2–3)

How does this excerpt from Brain change your perceptions about the poem? How does the notion of Plath's work as geographical help to explain the nature references in this poem? How are they overshadowed for you, as a reader, by that knowledge we all have of Plath's depression and death? Which of these two readings do you see as more applicable to this poem?

3. **Betrayal:** Does the daughter in this poem feel betrayed by her father?

Do you see betrayal as a driving force in this poem? Plath writes in her journals that she actually felt betrayed by her mother after her father died: "She came home crying like an angel one night and woke me up and told me Daddy was gone, he was what they called dead, and we'd never see him again, but the three of us would stick together and have a jolly life anyhow, to spite his face" (Kukil 430). Do you see these feelings about her mother in this poem? How does this sentiment from Plath's journal help to explain or complicate the reference to the *Oresteia*?

Form and Genre

Plath is usually considered a confessional poet. Most often, though, people think of what are usually considered the darker poems from the *Ariel* collection when they think of her confessional poetry. As you read through "The Colossus" and the following ideas, you might want to think about what you know about Plath's life and her background, what you think you know about her life, and what you need to know about her life in order to fully understand how this poem relates to her own experiences. Be careful of assuming too readily that everything Plath writes is autobiographical and that it all points to her mental illness. In order to understand the form and genre of this poem, you need to look at it as a piece of writing first and then look at it as a reflection of Plath's life and experiences.

Sample Topics:

1. **Confessional poetry:** Do you think this poem is a good example of confessional poetry? How does it fit the conventions of the genre?

   There is room in every discussion of poetry and literature for disagreement. How might you argue that this poem is not actually a confessional poem? Is there another genre of poetry that you think it more closely fits? The poem obviously deals with a daughter's loss of her father, so that is one fairly certain element of Plath's own experience entering into the poem. Where do you see her addressing larger issues in this poem? What would you argue is the main point Plath is making in this poem? If you see this poem as a solid example of confessional poetry, what specific lines or images in the poem would you use to support that assertion?

2. **Humor:** Where do you see Plath employing humor and word play in this poem?

Plath's poems are typically seen as serious, dark pieces. "The Colossus," though, is an example of the poet's ability to include humor and wordplay in her work. Where do you see Plath attempting to employ that "witty, wry, American, brazen, arrogant and, at times, comic" (Wagner-Martin, *Biography* 165) voice mentioned earlier in the chapter? Lynda Bundtzen argues that "Plath skillfully evokes the child's world with her own versions of Mother Goose rhymes" (Bundtzen 93) in much of her poetry. Do you see that happening here? One example might be when "The oracle utters only carnivalesque animal noises . . . which mock the idea of 'Tradition' as a repository of divine authority" (Britzolakis 180). Where else do you see Plath mocking or poking gentle fun at serious traditions? What do you think she is trying to do by incorporating these less-than-serious elements into a poem about trying to rebuild a life with her father?

3. **Stanzas:** How would you describe the arrangement of the stanzas in the poem? Are they arranged chronologically? Episodically?

How do you see the formation of the stanzas in this poem as helping to tell the story of the daughter's efforts to rebuild the colossus? Do you see any sort of timeline in the arrangement? What sort of rhythm is established by the five-line stanzas in this poem? What might you say is the rhyme scheme of this poem? Even though there are no traditional rhymes, what patterns do you see in word choices and line endings that help to establish a specific sound pattern? Reading the poem out loud will help you to gain a better understanding of how the stanzas and line endings affect the poem's meaning. Why do you think Plath used a five-line stanza form rather than the three-line form she often used?

Language, Symbolism, and Imagery

Sylvia Plath loved to play with words; she loved her thesaurus but at this time in her career was trying to make her language more colloquial and less academic sounding:

She had come to think of the poet as song-maker, not as scholar with her head buried in books. Plath did not break the thesaurus habit overnight but in 1959 she was working much more orally, listening to the language of the poem to see whether it was the language of speech. She was choosing her 'book poems,' those that would appear in her current collection [*The Colossus*], as much for the ease and naturalness of their language as for their subject matter. (Wagner-Martin, *Biography* 167).

As you think about a paper topic related to imagery and language in this poem, consider Plath's desire to make her work sound more conversational, even more approachable.

There are many references in this poem that are obviously related to ancient ruins and mythology; one scholar sees the poem as "an academic study of Greek and Roman architectural styles ('fluted bones,' 'acanthine hair')" (Britzolakis 179). When you are deciding on a topic for an essay, be careful of simply restating that fact and think about the how and the why. Especially for a student who might not be familiar with some of the references, a more detailed look at definitions and background information could yield some great ideas for exploring this poem and helping you arrive at an effective paper topic.

Sample Topics:

1. **Mythology:** Why do you think Plath chooses the specific mythological references she makes in the poem? What is she trying to communicate about her relationship with her father with those references?

   Judith Kroll sees Plath's familiarity with dying god and mourning goddess myths as surfacing in this poem, where "one dies and the survivor mourns and often searches for the lost 'underground' partner, who is eventually reborn" (84). How does this type of myth fit with Plath's feelings about her deceased father? What form does her mourning take in this poem? When the speaker "tends the ruined monolithic remains of her dead father" in this poem, how does she fulfill the role of a kind of cult priestess? (Kroll 84). In her journals, Plath refers to "my father-sea-god-muse" (Kukil 399). How does the definition of a muse as one of the nine daughters of Zeus (rather than the more modern definition of a muse as a source of inspiration) work in this poem? How does colossus serve as muse for the speaker in this poem?

2. **The natural realm:** What images of nature in this poem stand out to you as particularly worthy of note? What do they mean?

   Would you say that this poem is set outdoors or indoors? What in the poem makes you answer the way you do? What word choices does Plath make that help to heighten the idea of the colossus as being exposed to the elements? What emotions does this evoke in readers? In this poem, Plath writes that she hides from the wind in the ear of the colossus; she also notes that the sounds coming from the lips of the colossus are animal sounds. Do you think there is a connection between animal sounds coming from his lips and the fact that Otto Plath studied bumblebees? The speaker crawls across "weedy acres" and has lunch on "a hill of black cypress" and watches the stars and the sun from her perch on the colossus; what is the effect of having the colossus identified with these natural settings?

3. **Archaeology:** Britzolakis writes "the colossus . . . is both an architectural ruin and a dismembered body which the speaker desperately longs to reconstruct" (179). Why would Plath choose this metaphor as the driving force in the poem?

   What is significant about the idea of an archaeological dig that seems fitting for this exploration of a daughter's feelings for her deceased father? Bundtzen points out that "The archaeologist-daughter displays contradictory emotions toward the huge statue she is restoring. At first, she seems totally exasperated with the father and his godlike proportions and pretensions," but by the end of the poem she has taken a more worshipful stance (187–88). Why the change of heart? Where do you see the turning point in these emotions, and what do you see as responsible for it? How might that relate to what the daughter is really digging up? What exactly is being reassembled? Is it her life before he died? His life? Is the daughter intent on restoring him or his image?

4. **The oracle:** How does this colossus fit the definition of an oracle? What is it the speaker hopes to learn from the reassembled colossus? What knowledge does he have that she needs?

Linda Wagner-Martin writes, "As the poet mends the statue, she regards it as an oracle, the source of wisdom she desperately needs but cannot quite understand" (*Biography* 166). Why do you think it is so difficult for the daughter to understand what the colossus is saying? Does she hold herself responsible for her inability to understand him? Bundtzen writes, "This disparity between what the daughter knows and what she does with her life . . . deprives the daughter of any motive other than self-punishment for her devotion, and it appears to be entirely conscious" (188). How is this self-punishment presented in this poem? Based on how Plath has presented the colossus, do you think he would agree that she deserves to be punished?

Compare and Contrast Essays

Since this poem comes from her earliest published collection, it makes sense to base a compare and contrast essay on an examination of this poem and one of her later works. Plath's husband, Ted Hughes, saw three phases in his wife's work—her juvenilia, the *Colossus* phase (1956–1960), and the *Ariel* phase (from 1960 to her death). Because Plath has gained such posthumous fame, work from all three of these phases is readily available, so using the poems from these different phases of her writing could prove quite useful when writing a compare and contrast essay. Also, keeping in mind the influences Plath had from her husband and other poets of the time could offer you valuable ideas for a writing project.

Sample Topics:

1. **Compare "The Colossus" to "Daddy":** What are the biggest differences you notice in the way the father is portrayed in these poems? What are the similarities?

Kroll argues that in late poems, like "Daddy," the emotions Plath reveals seem like "sudden revelations" (86) when it can be argued that some of the motifs in her poetry, like that of her dead father, are actually present in her earlier work as well. How do you see the shift between both the speaker and the father figure between "The Colossus" and "Daddy"? How does the inclusion of a husband in "Daddy" affect the speaker's view of her father? How do you see the breakup of her marriage influencing her feelings about her father in the latter poem? Do you see a progression or a regression in the speaker's attitude toward her father from one poem to another? In "The Colossus," the daughter is trying to reassemble her father. Has she accomplished that in "Daddy," or is she still in the process of putting him back together? What is the significance of the daughter trying to unearth the father figure in "The Colossus" and burying him in "Daddy"? How do you think Plath wants readers to see the man in each of the poems?

2. **The absent father in "The Colossus" and in *The Bell Jar*:** How do you see the feelings associated with the absent father in the poem reflected in the novel?

In *The Bell Jar*, Esther's father dies when she is very young, as Plath's father did. At one point, Esther decides that she should start tending his grave; it is after that visit to his grave that she decides how she will kill herself. Does the speaker in the poem seem driven to self-destruction by her decision to reassemble her father? How does Esther's decision to revisit her father and tend to his grave compare to the meticulous effort the speaker in "The Colossus" puts into re-creating her father? Do Esther and the speaker in "The Colossus" have the same goals in piecing their fathers together? How would you describe the differences and similarities in the feelings the two characters have about their absent fathers? Do Esther's feelings seem like a progression from those of the speaker in "The Colossus"?

3. **The images in the poem to artwork by Giorgio de Chirico.**
How do you see paintings like de Chirico's *The Song of Love* or
Piazza d'Italia influencing Plath in "The Colossus"?

Sylvia Plath was an avid visual artist before she focused
her efforts on writing poetry, and many of the techniques
she learned in painting and sketching carried over into her
writing. She writes in her journals that she was particularly
inspired by Giorgio de Chirico and that his work moved her
(Britzolakis 167). Britzolakis also notes, "A number of Plath's
poems [including "The Colossus"] revolve around de Chiri-
coesque conceits such as the abandoned statue . . . the physical diminution of the speaker-figure . . . and the casting of
shadows" (168). What specific images in this poem support
this statement? How, with words, does Plath simulate a piece
of visual art in this poem? What do you think is the significance of the statues, or colossi, in the paintings and in Plath's
poem? How does the reference to ancient statuary work in
conjunction with the desolate landscapes against which they
are set?

4. **Work by Robert Lowell:** How does Lowell's poem "Father's
Bedroom" compare to "The Colossus"?

In her journals, Plath wrote of Lowell that she "had oddly a
similar reaction (excitement, joy, admiration, curiosity to
meet & praise) as when I first read Ted's poems" (Kukil 379).
She also attended a poetry workshop conducted by him and
even hosted him and his wife for dinner (Kukil 465). Where
in her poetry do you see the influence of Robert Lowell? How
does Plath build on the confessional style of Lowell? Do you
see this poem as a kind of homage to Lowell's work? Could you
argue that Plath is feminizing Lowell's confessional style with
this poem? In what other of Lowell's poems (especially from
the collection *Life Studies,* in which he writes of his father) do
you see the seeds of "The Colossus"?

Bibliography and Online Resources for "The Colossus"

Brain, Tracy. *The Other Sylvia Plath*. Harlow, England: Pearson, 2001. Print.

"A Brief Guide to Confessional Poetry." *Poets.org*. The Academy of American Poets. n.d. Web. 15 Aug. 2010.

Britzolakis, Christine. "Conversation among the Ruins." *Eye Rhymes: Sylvia Plath's Art of the Visual*. Kathleen Connors and Sally Bayley, Eds. Oxford: Oxford U P, 2007. Print.

Bundtzen, Lynda. *Plath's Incarnations: Woman and the Creative Process*. Ann Arbor: U of Michigan P, 1983. Print.

Butscher, Edward. *Sylvia Plath: Method and Madness*. New York: Seabury P, 1976. Print.

Kroll, Judith. *Chapters in a Mythology: The Poetry of Sylvia Plath*. New York: Harper and Row, 1976. Print.

Kukil, Karen V. *The Unabridged Journals of Sylvia Plath*. New York: Anchor Books, 2001.

Plath, Sylvia. "The Colossus." *The Colossus and Other Poems*. 1957. New York: Vintage International, 1998. Print.

Wagner-Martin, Linda. *Sylvia Plath: A Biography*. New York: Simon and Schuster, 1987. Print.

———. *Sylvia Plath: A Literary Life*. Hampshire, England: Macmillan P, 1999. Print.

"THE MOON AND THE YEW TREE"

READING TO WRITE

"The Moon and the Yew Tree" was originally published in the collection titled *Ariel,* which came out in 1965, two years after Sylvia Plath's death. Many critics agree that it is one of Plath's best poems. She wrote it in October 1961, when she and her husband, Ted Hughes, were living in Court Green, an "ancient manor-cum-rectory in North Devon [England] where she was to write the poems that made her famous" (Stevenson 221). When she read this poem, along with several others, to her friend and fellow writer Al Alvarez, he "concluded that she was developing something 'strong and new' in her work" (Alexander 304), a sentiment shared by many critics. Devon plays an important role in the new voice in the poetry Plath wrote during the last few years of her life, as is evidenced by many of the images in this poem.

Across the street from Court Green was an Anglican church that offered Plath a significant amount of inspiration for her work. According to Anne Stevenson, a noted Plath biographer, the impetus for "The Moon and the Yew Tree" came from Ted, who "had set her the subject as an exercise after they observed the full moon setting over the yew in the churchyard early one morning" (229). Although a successful work for Plath, Hughes later noted of the poem, "It depressed me greatly" (Stevenson 229).

Once again it is essential to not read the poem solely as a harbinger of Plath's suicide. Reading the poem as a work purposefully created by Plath to evoke certain reactions or emotions in readers is a better way to approach it than seeing it as evidence that she was depressed. The poem was written during an especially productive time in Plath's career, the fall of 1961, a year and a half before her death. Stevenson notes the success of the poem and also notes Plath's own reaction to the work:

> The most outstanding of the poems Sylvia wrote in September and October 1961 is 'The Moon and the Yew Tree.' Speaking of it on the radio in July 1962, Sylvia remarked that the yew tree had taken the poem over completely, as with 'astounding egotism' it proceeded to 'manage and order the whole affair.' (229)

Aside from the title, the yew tree is only mentioned specifically twice in the poem, which might make it easy for a reader to underestimate its significance in the poem. This is where a different set of reading skills than you use for reading a novel or short story becomes helpful. Poems can seem daunting to readers because things like themes and philosophy are not always as readily identifiable as they are in prose writing. But once you get some practice reading poetry, finding solid ideas for essays is not as hard as it may seem.

With this in mind, a reader can begin to set aside the urge to read the poem for signs of distress on Plath's part, thinking instead, perhaps, of how the yew tree becomes the dominant figure in the work. A close reading of the last stanza of the poem yields some insight into Plath's comments:

> I have fallen a long way. Clouds are flowering
> Blue and mystical over the face of the stars.
> Inside the church, the saints will all be blue,
> Floating on their delicate feet over the cold pews,
> Their hands and faces stiff with holiness.
> The moon sees nothing of this. She is bald and wild.
> And the message of the yew tree is blackness—blackness
> and silence. (22–28)

Throughout the poem the yew tree is a major presence, dark and towering and serving as a sort of anchor for the speaker. While the clouds, the saints, and the moon are movable and unpredictable, the yew tree is staid; it points to the moon (15), but it does not move. And its final message, of blackness and silence, suggests immobility untouched by moonlight or the movements of the saints. The shadowy nature of the yew tree could be reflective of Plath's feelings about her deceased father, as well. Several critics and biographers suggest that Plath is referencing her parents in this poem: "There are two pairs of parental figures in this poem: the mother and father as the moon and yew tree, who punish and are indifferent to her pain; and the icons of the church, Mary and the saints, who offer forgiveness and holiness" (Bundtzen 200). Since her father is gone, he is no longer a static figure; instead, he is fixed and mute, not unlike the yew tree. The final words of the poem about the yew tree's message of "blackness and silence" also indicate the silence of Plath's father after his death.

This is just one way to read this stanza. As you reread the poem and find particular pieces of it that speak to you, consider what statement you think Plath is making with this poem. Is she making a personal statement about her parents? About her own parenting? Or do you see her making statements about bigger issues like religion or even politics? While there are what may be called "preferred" readings of poems like this—and especially well-known ones—there are many ways that this poem can be read and interpreted in effective and interesting ways.

TOPICS AND STRATEGIES

This section of the chapter is meant to offer you some ways to look at "The Moon and the Yew Tree" and to offer some suggestions that can help you decide what you want to write about Plath's poem. This is not meant to be a comprehensive list of "approved" topics, though. Instead, think of the ideas presented here as tools you can use to unearth or enhance your own ideas about the poem. As you read the poem, note which lines, images, words, or other points stand out to you for some reason. Let the strategies included here help you decide how to write about those reactions you have to the poem.

Remember, too, that in order to better understand and appreciate a poem, it is important to read it several times and also to read it out loud. Many poets, including Plath, are adamant that their work be read aloud; she "reproached [Al] Alvarez, who wanted to read them silently.

These poems must be read *aloud* she said" (Alexander 303). As you read through this and other poems discussed in this volume, think about why this was so important to Plath and how that might affect how you write about her work.

Themes

Identifying a theme or themes in a poem can be especially difficult, because it can seem like there's not enough of a story in a poem to really develop a theme. But as you read a poem again and think about what the poet is saying through the images and word choices he or she makes, themes can begin to emerge more clearly. In this poem, for instance, there are many references to church and religion; "The grasses unload their griefs on my feet as if I were God" (3) and "Twice on Sunday, the bells startle the sky— / Eight great tongues affirming the Resurrection" (12–13) are just two examples of this. As you look for a theme to write about, think about how you would explain the poem to someone who has not read it. What would you say the poem is about? Answering that question and thinking about how you would interpret the poem can help you to identify a theme that you can explore in a paper or an essay.

Sample Topics:

1. **Religion:** What do you think Plath is saying about religion in this poem?

   Since this poem is set in a churchyard, religion is obviously a significant element of the work. What specific references to religion or church do you see? How does Plath develop those references to make a statement about religion? Is she comforted by the churchyard across the street or disturbed by it? One biographer argues, "'I live here,' is a separate statement that applies both to the town and to . . . despair. Religion does not help; the church bells ring out twice on Sunday to affirm 'the Resurrection,' but conclude 'soberly' on 'their names' in a pathetic plea for identity" (Butscher 297). How do you see this idea as an accurate reading of the poem or, conversely, what alternate readings do you see?

2. **Family:** What is Plath saying about her family in this poem? What is she saying about her own role in her family?

Several critics and biographers see the moon in this poem as Plath's own mother and the yew tree as her father. What are her feelings toward her parents, based on your reading of this poem? Does she resent her father for dying? Her mother for living? What influence does her father, as symbolized by the yew tree, still exert on her? How do the moon and the yew tree influence how the poet sees each of them? How do the moon and the yew tree interact and/or fit together? Are they in opposition, or are they working in collaboration? Since the poet had two children at the time she wrote the poem, could you argue that Plath is writing about herself as a mother and about Hughes as a father?

3. **Life and death:** What is Plath saying about the tension between life and death in this poem? Which seems preferable to her?

One biographer sees this in the poem: "Traditionally, yew trees are associated with death, so the very title of the poem is setting out the major opposition of extremes—moon . . . *versus* the yew tree" (Butscher 297). Which of the two, the moon or the yew tree, does Plath see as more threatening? According to many legends, the yew tree can also symbolize life because it is so hardy and long-lived. How does this complicate or clarify how you read the yew tree's role in this poem? What is the significance of the "row of headstones" (6)? How is that significance affected by the reference to the bells "affirming the Resurrection?" (13) Could you argue that the theme of death in this poem would not seem so obvious if Plath had not killed herself? How are readers' perceptions about death images in this poem influenced by Plath's own death?

4. **Freedom and imprisonment:** Does Plath feel imprisoned by what she sees in the churchyard, or does she feel locked out of a place she wishes to get to?

Anne Stevenson argues that "Inevitably, the churchyard with its father-yew and mother-moon had become yet another reen-actment of Sylvia's imprisoning drama" (229). What do you believe is imprisoning Plath in this poem? Do you see this poem as an attempt to escape that prison? Conversely, Bundtzen argues, "Because of her despair, the speaker cannot believe in the church as a refuge" (200). Remember in the first chapter of this book Plath's attempts to join the church and her desire for Frieda to attend Sunday school are discussed. Do you believe the speaker in this poem wants to find refuge in the church? Is Plath looking for a way out or for a way in? Is she, as one author notes, "seeking a path into another world" that is denied her because 'The message of the yew tree is blackness—blackness and silence'" (Holbrook 158)? If so, what is that other world?

Characters

With poetry it is often more difficult than with novels to identify and discuss character. It can be helpful to set aside *some* of the reading habits you have developed reading fiction in order to work with poetry. By reading closely and using a little bit of imagination, pinpointing characters in a poem can be easier than you might think at first. For example, in this poem it seems safe to say there are three characters: the moon, the yew tree, and the speaker. Because Plath employs some personification in this poem, which is giving inanimate or non-human objects human characteristics, seeing a tree and the moon as characters is quite possible. Edward Butscher writes that Plath's husband saw his wife including herself in the poem, noting that Hughes "saw in the allegory of the lost little girl the pattern of night forces tearing away at Sylvia's soul" (Butscher 297). Think of this connection to Plath as you consider writing about the speaker in this poem, especially.

Sample Topics:

1. **The moon:** Is Plath's mother the only person or being symbolized by the moon in this poem? If it is symbolic of her mother, based on her representation of the moon in this poem, what is she saying about her?

What else or who else could be signified by the moon in this poem? What do you see as the most or least compelling argument for the moon symbolizing Plath's mother? Although the moon does not utter any words in this poem, is it still communicating something? If so, what? Is the message solely for the speaker of the poem? In *Letters Home*, a compilation of letters Sylvia Plath sent to her mother, Aurelia, the relationship between mother and daughter seems strong and amicable. How can a reader of both reconcile the good-natured correspondence between the poet and her mother and the portrayal of the moon in this poem? Where do you see the speaker's feelings about the moon being expressed in the poem? What are those feelings?

2. **The yew:** Is Plath's father the only person or thing symbolized by the yew tree in this poem? If it is symbolic of her father, based on her representation of the yew tree in this poem, what is she saying about him?

What else or who else could be signified by the yew tree in this poem? There are many legends surrounding the yew tree, from its usefulness in making weapons to its longevity to its equation with death. Research some of these legends and decide which you think most appropriately reflects Plath's intentions in this poem. Do you think the yew tree is preventing the speaker from seeing "where there is to get to," (7) or is the yew tree part of what the speaker wants to get to? Where do you see the speaker's feelings about the yew tree being expressed in the poem? What are those feelings? Does the speaker fear the yew tree? Find strength in it? Does the yew tree take a dominant or subordinate position to the moon in this poem? While not overtly threatening, the tree is nonetheless a dark presence within the typically safe realm of a church. What do you think this means? What is Plath saying about whatever is embodied in the image of the yew tree?

3. **The speaker:** What role does the speaker of this poem play in the drama of the moon and the yew tree? Is the speaker more or less connected to either of them?

Is it necessary to imagine Plath as the speaker in this poem in order to interpret it? Plath often said her work should not be read as completely autobiographical. If you read the poem as *not* about Plath and her parents, does that change the message delivered by the speaker of this poem? Who, then, is the speaker? Is the speaker offering explanation or interpretation to readers? Trying to sway readers to see the moon and/or the yew tree in a specific way?

History and Context

The period in which Plath wrote this poem, October 1961, was a particularly fruitful one for her. She was living at Court Green in Devon with Ted and Frieda and was pregnant with Nicholas. Soon after moving to Devon, Sylvia attended the church next door to try to make a stronger connection with the village, writing to her mother that she thought it would be a good way to get to know people and that she would like Frieda to attend Sunday school there; she also noted that "The view of the church from the house was pretty" (Stevenson 225). Later, however, she wrote to her mother that she was uncomfortable with the politics of the church rector and had received some bad reactions to one of her stories from the parishioners (Stevenson 226). Her reaction to that sermon is likely tied to her political and social views. In a letter to her mother shortly after writing "The Moon and the Yew Tree," Sylvia expresses horror at talk of war and political unrest in the United States (Plath, Aurelia 438). She discusses at some length the various news stories she has read and heard on the BBC and her concerns about the possibility of war. Many of her biographers point out this penchant Plath had for keeping up with current events, and many readers see this interest in politics and other world issues in her writing. As you think about what to write for your project, keep this in mind.

Sample Topics:

1. **The cold war:** What political statements might Plath be making in this poem?

How might Plath be using the moon and the yew tree to make statements about communism and democracy? What images and references in the poem could be read as commentary, or even expressions of fear, from Plath about the political climate in the world at this time? The early 1960s were a volatile period for relations between the United States (and its allies, including Great Britain) and communist countries like Cuba and Russia. How do you see this unrest being explored in this poem? What would it have been like for an American living abroad during this time period? Was public opinion in Great Britain sympathetic or unsympathetic to American positions against communism?

2. **Women's issues:** What might Plath be saying about women's issues in this poem? About her mother's role in her and her father's lives?

As discussed earlier in this book, the early 1960s were an important time for the women's rights movement. How does Plath address this in "The Moon and the Yew Tree"? How does Plath use the moon to illustrate some of those issues women were facing? Following the popular reading of the moon in this poem as symbolic of Plath's own mother, what do you think Plath is saying about her mother, Aurelia? Although the moon is the more mentioned figure, the yew tree "takes over" the poem; what might that say about Plath's views of the relationship between her mother and her father? How might some of the images in this poem reflect Plath's own feelings about her role as wife and mother?

3. **Country versus city life:** How could this poem demonstrate Plath's feelings about living in the country? What images and references here seem specific to the rural lifestyle Plath was living at the time?

One Plath biographer notes of the moon imagery in this poem: "Interestingly, the moon, which was always a favorite image of Plath's, reappears with more frequency again in her work when she moved to the country where the city lights did not interfere with her view of it" (Kirk 111). What else in this poem do you see as representative of Plath's life in the country? Do you see anything in this poem that could be read as a statement about which is preferable—life in the country or life in the city? The moon and yew trees can be seen in the city as well as in the country; how is Plath's treatment of them here more resonant with the country than with the city?

Philosophy and Ideas

Plath says a lot about many major issues in this as well as in her other poems. One way to discern the philosophical message of a piece of writing is to decide what the writer is saying—not just about an issue or a theme but about life. In this poem, Plath is addressing a number of big issues, some of which have been discussed earlier in this chapter. One thing that seems particularly important for Plath in this poem is religion. Ronald Hayman writes that Plath talked with the rector at the Anglican Church where the yew tree stood, but "Her Unitarian past made it impossible for her to accept the idea of the Trinity." She attended a service and, although she enjoyed much about it, was "bored by the platitudinous sermon" (163). Hayman reads this poem as an example of how Plath "needs to feel she's going somewhere, needs comfort, needs to believe in tenderness, but, far from being a door, and far from being sweet, like Mary, the moon is a face, white and desperate, bald and wild, while the comfortless message of the yew is blackness and silence" (Hayman 163). Think of Plath looking across the street to this church—does Hayman's explanation make sense?

Sample Topics:

1. **Faith versus reason:** Is Plath struggling with her own feelings about church and religion here? As you reread the poem, what would you say about Plath's ideas about religion and faith?

   In this poem, Plath sees the light of the mind as "cold and planetary" (1). What do you think this means? How might this demonstrate some of the struggle Hayman writes about?

What does Plath mean when she writes, "I have fallen a long way" (22)? Do you think she's referencing the Fall from Bible stories? Of faith or reason, which do you think Plath sees as offering her the most comfort? Which do you see her saying has left her comfortless? If the moon and the yew tree are her parents, is one more tied to reason and one to faith? If so, which do you see tied to each (reason and faith)? Does Plath want to find comfort in the church, or is she decrying it for not offering her comfort because she thinks religion cannot offer that for anyone?

2. **Control:** Who has control in this poem—the moon? The yew tree? The poet/speaker? The saints in the church?

   Plath herself said the yew tree took over the poem, but that does not necessarily equate with control over the other elements in the work. Which images or lines in this poem seem to portray a struggle for control? What or who do you think is the object of the control—the poet? The moon or the yew tree? The readers? Is Plath arguing that religion controls believers' lives? If so, to what effect? What might she be saying about the control her parents have over her? If the yew tree does, indeed, take over the poem, could that be read as an indication that it, as a symbol of her father, is still in control of her family?

3. **Familial love:** What does the speaker want from the moon and the yew tree? How is that similar (or not) to what Plath wanted from her parents?

   One of the most common readings of this poem holds that the moon and the yew tree represent Plath's parents, Aurelia and Otto Plath. Reading the poem from that perspective, what is Plath saying about her relationships with her father and with her mother? What is lacking in those relationships? Based on her treatment of the yew tree in the poem, what is Plath saying about the affect of Otto's death on her family? Does she love her parents? What in the poem leads you to answer *yes* or *no*? How might this affect her as a mother? Is there anything in this poem that speaks to her relationship with her husband and her own children?

Form and Genre

Poetry comes in a variety of genres, including narrative, dramatic, lyric, and confessional. Because confessional poetry usually incorporates autobiographical elements (the poet "confessing" her or his true feelings through the poem), many readers see Plath's work, especially her late works such as "The Moon and the Yew Tree," as examples of the genre. One thing to keep in mind about confessional poetry is that it also requires the poet to take on a voice, so while there are certainly autobiographical elements included in a confessional poem, the poet is still working to create an image or images within the poem. What images do you see Plath creating here? There are references to church and Christianity in this poem; how might you explain the autobiographical connection to Plath? How do the church/religious references here make sense or not make sense in a confessional poem as opposed to another genre of poem?

One way to look at Plath's poetry is as works in progress. Plath was an enthusiastic and fervent reviser of her own works. Referring to *Ariel: The Restored Edition* would offer you opportunities to write about revisions Plath made to her poems because it features facsimiles of her manuscripts, complete with her handwritten revisions. How might you discuss some of those revisions in a paper? How might you argue that when readers look at previous versions of a particular poem they may see how Plath crafts images for effect rather than seeing merely a suicidal poet writing about her own depression? Can any of the revisions be explained more fully by referring to biographical works or Plath's journals?

Sample Topics:

1. **Confessional poetry:** How does this poem exemplify confessional poetry? Or how would you argue that it is not actually of that genre?

What conventions of confessional poetry does "The Moon and the Yew Tree" follow? Do you believe this poem is auto-biographical? Is it so overshadowed by Plath's suicide that it gets read as a confessional piece no matter what? What is Plath saying about herself in this poem? Plath was a student of Robert Lowell, a noted American poet known for his confessional poetry; how do you see this poem as influenced by Lowell's style? What exactly is Plath confessing in this poem? To whom is the speaker, and/or Plath, confessing? What is to be gained for the speaker (or the poet) by sharing these feelings? Is it hinted at or outlined in the poem?

2. **Rhythm:** How would you describe the rhythm of this poem?

The stanzas in this poem all have seven lines. Do you see a recognizable meter in the stanzas? If so, what is it and what is emphasized by that meter? If not, what does Plath do to make the poem flow? Reread the poem out loud; try it a few times. How does your understanding of the poem change when you read it out loud? Remember that Plath was insistent that her poems were meant to be read out loud. When you read it out loud, did you notice the emphasis on certain words or images shift from when you read it silently? Consider the punctuation in the poem; how does that lead readers through the words and images in the work?

3. **Voice:** Whose voice is being heard by readers in this poem?

Plath was an American, but she was living in England when she wrote this poem and many of the others that made her famous. Is the voice in this poem an American one or a British one? Plath was also a mother and a daughter—do you see one or both of those voices in this poem? What influences do you see from these different identities at play in this work? When you think about the theme or the overall message of the poem, how does the speaker's, or Plath's, voice bring out that message? Is

Plath trying to speak for herself in this poem? Is she speaking for anyone other than herself? How might you read this poem as a statement about a social or political issue?

Language, Symbols, and Imagery

This poem is laden with language, symbols, and imagery that offer possibilities for an essay. Needless to say, the two most important and most-discussed images in the poem are the moon and the yew tree. Exploring those two symbolic figures unravels subsequent images and symbols, as well. As Judith Kroll points out, "The moon . . . illuminates a wounded landscape of harsh contrasts—of light and shadow, often unnaturally brilliant, with a suggestion of the violent, the uncontrollable, or the supernatural" (32). Reading closely and examining the ways in which Plath characterizes these two figures in the poem can open other doors for investigation and consideration. Resist the temptation to overlook the other images and symbols in the poem because these are the most prominent; watch for important images like the cemetery and the bells, as well, because they are integral parts in understanding what Plath is doing with the moon and the yew tree here.

Plath also uses color to create a mood in this poem; "This four-stanza poem reveals Plath's late color preferences—minus red—and careful manipulation of dark and light contrasts in relation to associative color imagery" (Connors 133). Recalling Plath's skills in painting and drawing might also help you think about how she composed this piece.

Sample Topics:

1. **Dark and light:** How is the tension between dark and light used in this poem? What message does that tension convey?

How does Plath's use of light and dark in this poem reflect the visual art technique called chiaroscuro? Where does she rely on commonly held associations of light and dark with good and evil to make a statement in this poem? What statement is she making using the dark and the light? Why does Plath combine the descriptions of the lightness of the moon with violent words, such as saying it is "White as a knuckle" (9)? Note what is described in terms of lightness and what in darkness; do you see a pattern emerge? How can Plath incorporate so many important images of light in this poem and yet have so many readers see it as a dark poem? How does the darkness of the yew tree illustrate Plath's point about the yew tree taking over the poem?

2. **Color:** What do the colors Plath chooses to use in this poem communicate to readers? What is the significance of the emphasis on black and white and blue?

In a letter to her mother in 1961, Plath writes, "I am so suggestible to colors and textures that I'm sure a red carpet would keep me forever optimistic" (Plath, Aurelia 435). How do the colors in this poem illustrate this suggestibility she talks about? What associations does she make between certain colors and certain emotions? What is the significance of having so many religious elements of the poem, like the saints and the moon's garments, in blue? What words does Plath use in this poem that bring to mind certain colors even if she does not mention a color specifically? How does color (or the lack of it) contribute to the mood of this poem?

3: **Nature:** How does Plath use nature images in this poem? Is she trying to evoke certain emotions in readers?

What images from nature, including the moon and the yew tree, does Plath rely on in this poem? How does she manipulate the natural to create analogies or metaphors? As Kroll points out, "The visual appearance of the Moon itself is often invested with female attributes" (34); what other inanimate objects does Plath invest with human attributes? Why use images from nature to symbolize her mother and father? Does

Plath find any solace in the natural world she sees as she ponders the yew tree and the moon? Does the wildness of the moon and the yew tree frighten her? How does the juxtaposition of nature and the church work to describe Plath's own feelings about religion? Which takes precedence for Plath—nature or the church?

4. **The body:** What is the significance of Plath's references to body parts? How does the use of body imagery work to humanize, or even dehumanize, the moon and the yew tree?

Which parts of the body are mentioned in this poem? Why do you think Plath chose as she did? How does Plath incorporate the five senses into this poem? Is one more highly developed than the others? How do those physical senses help to create a mental state of despair? One critic writes, "The radiance of the moon, the threatening shadows of the yew tree, and the bruiselike combination of black and blue are composed into a mental landscape of 'complete despair'" (Bundtzen 200–01); could you argue that Plath's choice of words and images signifies a sort of physical assault? What injury comes to the speaker by having "fallen a long way" (22)?

Compare and Contrast Essays

A big part of writing a successful compare and contrast essay is choosing carefully what to compare and/or contrast. In Plath's case, one obvious approach might be to consider her earlier work and her later work. Since her journals and letters have been published, you also have the luxury of looking at what she wrote to herself as well as to her mother and her brother and comparing that to the poetry she wrote. For example, in a letter to her mother written about the time she wrote this poem, Sylvia writes, "I've decided the best way to grow into the community here is to go to our local Anglican church. . . . I like the idea of Frieda going to Sunday School next door. . . . The church . . . has a champion crew of eight bellringers who delight us every Sunday" (Plath, Aurelia 432). One idea for an essay might be to think about how the tone of this letter either melds with or alters or contrasts with the images of the same church presented in "The Moon and the Yew Tree."

Sample Topics:

1. **Plath's letters and journals compared to her published work:** Compare and contrast what Plath wrote to her mother and brother with the tone of the published works she writes about.

   Choose some letters Plath wrote to her mother and/or her brother about the time she was writing this poem. How can a reader reconcile the tone of the letters Sylvia sent to her mother (upbeat about the church, its bells, etc.) and the tone of the published version of this poem (considered to be dark and foreboding)? Does one voice feel more authentic to you than the other? Read through some of Plath's journal entries from this time of her life; can you identify specific references or influences or inspirations for this poem? If you compare her letters and her journals, do you see anything that you feel is contradictory?

2. **"The Moon and the Yew Tree" and works by other writers:** Compare and contrast this poem with poems by a writer or writers who had an influence on Plath and her writing.

   What specific images in this poem can you identify as inspired by other writers? Kroll argues that moon images and colors in Robert Graves's book *The White Goddess* were a major influence on Plath as she wrote this and other poems (41). She also points out that "Plath was familiar with many of the writings and contexts [of Yeats] in which the Moon is associated with mind" (206). In what ways can you see these specific influences in this poem? What other influences do you see in this work? Ted Hughes gave Plath the seed for this poem by urging her to write about the yew tree. Choose a poem by Hughes ("The Laburnum Top" might be a good choice) and consider the influences you see each of them having on the other. You might also consider choosing a poem written after Plath (such as one from the collection *The Plath Cabinet*) and compare or contrast her work with that of other poets inspired and influenced by her.

3. **"Elm" and "Edge":** Compare and contrast these poems with "The Moon and the Yew Tree."

How do you see earlier works by Plath leading up to this poem? What important images or words that appear in earlier works are repeated in this poem? One critic argues, "'Elm' is a fine poem, though uneven, uncertain of its voice and narrative focus, a rehearsal, a final dress rehearsal for 'The Moon and the Yew Tree'" (Butscher 196). Kroll also points out that one phase of moon imagery for Plath starts here and ends with the moon in "Edge" (44). Read the two poems and compare the moon imagery in them. Do you agree with Kroll's assertion? Disagree? Discuss how, using specific images and lines from the poems to support your ideas.

Bibliography and Online Resources for "The Moon and the Yew Tree"

Alexander, Paul. *Rough Magic: A Biography of Sylvia Plath.* New York: DeCapo, 1999. Print.

Bowman, Catherine. *The Plath Cabinet.* New York: Four Way Books, 2009. Print.

Bundtzen, Lynda. *Plath's Incarnations: Woman and the Creative Process.* Ann Arbor, MI: U of MI P, 1983. Print.

Butscher, Edward. *Sylvia Plath: Method and Madness.* New York: Seabury P, 1976. Print.

Hayman, Ronald. *The Death and Life of Sylvia Plath.* New York: Carol, 1991.

Kirk, Connie Ann. *Sylvia Plath: A Biography.* Amherst, NY: Prometheus, 2009. Print.

Kroll, Judith. *Chapters in a Mythology: The Poetry of Sylvia Plath.* New York: Harper and Row, 1976. Print.

Plath, Sylvia. *Ariel: The Restored Edition.* London: Faber and Faber, 2004.

———. "The Moon and the Yew Tree." *The Collected Poems: Sylvia Plath*. Ted Hughes, Ed. New York: Harper Perennial, 2008. Print.

Stevenson, Anne. *Bitter Fame: A Life of Sylvia Plath*. Boston: Mariner Books, 1989. Print.

"ARIEL"

READING TO WRITE

"Ariel" was written on Sylvia Plath's last birthday, October 27, 1962. The poem is the namesake of Plath's most famous and widely read collection, *Ariel,* which was published after her death in 1965. This collection is undoubtedly Plath's most famous and critically acclaimed, helping earn her the Pulitzer Prize in 1982 for *The Collected Poems,* nearly 20 years after her death. Almost certainly much of the interest in the collection stemmed from the sensation created by Plath's suicide. The tone of the poems in this collection is striking—unlike the more wry tone of *The Colossus* and the still-forming voice in *Crossing the Water,* the poems in *Ariel* are strong, strident, and full of what has become accepted as Plath's own brand of confessional poetry.

As with much of Plath's poems, many readers see a lot of autobiographical details in "Ariel." Both because of that fact and in spite of it, this poem can be more difficult to read than some of Plath's other well-known works. "Ariel" is one of several poems in the collection of the same name ("Lady Lazarus" is another) that feature a three-line stanza format. In this poem especially, the format highlights a distinctive rhythm that is often likened to a ride on a horse. As Pamela Annas argues, the poem can be read as "[l]iterally an account of a gallop on a horse named Ariel" in which "the poet escapes the cycle of death and rebirth and becomes transformed into something bodiless though not dispersed" (127). The images in the poem are also quite powerful and address some themes that are not uncommon in Plath's work. For instance, Claire Brennan sees the movement of the poem as helping to make a strong feminist statement, noting, "In 'Ariel,' Plath is the most reckless in enacting her poetics through the fiery transubstantiation of the female subject" (110). Judith Kroll is one of many critics who note a plethora of mythological references.

Because these themes and images are seen in other work by Plath, readers can sometimes automatically assume this poem is saying the same thing the poet says in other poems. But while the poem contains many of Plath's recognizable treatments of issues in this poem, it is important to see it as a discrete piece that, although part of a collection, has a life of its own. In many ways "Ariel" is different from Plath's other well-recognized poetry. Several critics who note this difference point to the rhythm and stanza arrangement, arguing there is a strong influence from Emily Dickinson in this poem. And while many readers (and even some critics) read much of Plath's poetry as an indication of her impending suicide, this poem is infused with a much more defiant tone; "Ariel" does not have in it some of the pointed references to depression and suicide some of her other works from this collection contain. As you read through the work and start to formulate ideas for an essay, consider both the ways this poem seems to reflect ideas in her other works as well as how it is unique compared to other of her works you have read.

Whenever you write about poetry, it is important to read the work out loud in order to get a truer feel for the rhythm of the work, which can help you interpret the work more effectively. In this case, reading the poem to yourself is essential to helping you unearth some rich ideas for essays. Take the following excerpt from the poem as an example:

> Something else
> Hauls me through air—
>
> Thighs, hair;
> Flakes from my heels.
>
> White
> Godiva, I unpeel—
> Dead hands, dead stringencies.

And now I
Foam to wheat, a glitter of seas.
The child's cry

Melts in the wall. (15–25)

Especially when you read it out loud, you can hear how the cadence of the poem mirrors that of a ride on a horse, as Annas notes. The purposeful punctuation and separation of lines also forces readers to recognize powerful movement, carried along at a sort of gallop by the stanza breaks. Plath would have been familiar with the feeling of riding a horse; while living at Court Green, she took lessons at a stable near their home on a horse named Ariel (Kroll 180). In this excerpt, the assertion that the speaker is carried by "Something else" lends credence to the idea that the speaker is riding some sort of mythical creature, equine or otherwise. This ride, however, is more than a simple horseback ride—it is a ride to destiny, a ride that carries the speaker away from the earthly toward the divine.

Another notable element of this poem is the idea that the speaker is shedding things as she rides; this ride is liberating her as she "unpeels" what is dead from her. Even a child's cry melts away as the speaker shoots toward "the red / Eye, the cauldron of morning" (30–31), the sun. The trajectory the speaker takes allows her to get rid of all that is earthly, including parts of her self, as she catapults from the world into space. Readers can see how Plath is moving the speaker of the poem from the dark, in the first line of the poem, into the ultimate light, the sun, by the end of the poem. The ride is wild, but not uncontrolled, because the rider realizes what is happening as she moves forward, she sees what she is letting go and what she is moving toward, so there is a sense of empowerment in her voice.

TOPICS AND STRATEGIES

Deciding on topics for writing about poetry can sometimes seem much more difficult than finding topics to write about for novels or longer works. However, when you keep in mind that poetry is just as purposefully engineered as prose, it can help you see possible topics. One thing to remember is that it is important to carefully consider each word and each line in a poem; it can be easy to read through a poem quickly and think to yourself, "I don't get it." Do not despair if you feel that you do not see anything to write about after one reading; as you get more familiar with the work by rereading it, you will start to notice details that will help you choose possible topics for more research or consideration.

One more thing to think about as you mull over possible topics for an essay is that just because you see a theme or an image or a character in this work that you see in other works by Plath, do not assume it is being treated in the same way. Basically, be careful of discounting a possible topic for a paper because you think it is just another example of something. The poet made a purposeful decision to include whatever it is you are looking at in the poem, so as a writer it is up to you to think about why. Use the following ideas for writing about "Ariel" as tools for you to figure out what you see in the poem and what you want to say about it. These ideas do not represent a comprehensive list of topics, but some of them might make you see the poem differently, which can help you break through writer's block and come up with a successful idea for an essay.

Themes

Some of the themes in this poem are obvious, but there are others that might not jump out at you as quickly. The following ideas for themes are not unfamiliar ones in Plath's work, yet it is important to think about how they are specifically treated in this poem. "Ariel" can seem deceptively slim in terms of ideas for papers because it is fairly short and can be challenging to understand, yet there are countless subtleties and interpretations that offer ideas for essays that move beyond what might seem like obvious images and references.

One thing to keep in mind as you read this poem is the way that you, as a student in the twenty-first century, read this poem compared to how it would have been received when it was first published in the early 1960s. Keep in mind that Plath's suicide had gained her instant fame—a fame some argue she might not have achieved had she not brought about her own death. For almost everyone reading Plath for the first time *now*, her sensational death is an integral part of her poetry. Try to set that knowledge aside as you think about writing projects related to this poem;

consider the poem as a piece of writing designed to raise eyebrows and bring up themes that were not commonly addressed as they are now.

Sample Topics:

1. **Finding the true self:** How does this journey help the speaker find her true self? Where do you see the speaker discovering her true identity?

In this poem, the rider is shedding things as she goes, moving into the burning cauldron; fire becomes a purifying force for her (Kroll 181). Why is this ride necessary for the speaker? Do you think this ride toward the cauldron is one that the speaker planned, or is it something that she has been caught up in unwittingly? How does the progression from darkness in the first line to the White Godiva (19–20) to the red eye (30–31) illustrate the speaker's progression toward self-realization? What do the things she sheds along the way show about who the speaker was and who she will become?

2. **Death:** Is death tragic in this poem or redemptive? How is death reached in this poem?

Lynda Bundtzen argues that:

> Despite the mood of despair and tragic fatality in [several of Plath's] poems . . . Plath resists as often as she surrenders to self-destructive impulses. Ambivalence is her habitual attitude, so that even where death looks like a state of repose, ease, or perfection itself . . . there is an underlying tension that is the sign of an ongoing conflict" (36).

Is the speaker in this poem being self-destructive when she becomes the "dew that flies / Suicidal" (28–29) into the burning cauldron, or is she saving herself? Bundtzen writes the dew is suicidal simply because it evaporates, so the reference to suicide does not necessarily indicate desire on Plath's part to die (10). Does the speaker believe that all of her must die or just the parts of her she sheds along the way? What does death accomplish for her?

3. **Inner conflict for the woman as artist:** What images or references in this poem point to the tension between typical women's roles and the woman as artist?

Linda Wagner-Martin notes, "Just as so many of Plath's journal entries dealt with her future work, and the conundrum of which work a talented woman writer, artist, and teacher should take up, so many of her poems deal with the varieties of achieving women" (*Literary Life* 106). What roles of women is the speaker trying to escape? How do the things she unpeels from herself and the things she leaves behind illustrate your answer? Why is the "red / Eye, the cauldron of morning" (30–31) her target? What does the speaker in this poem achieve, or what does she hope to achieve? Does stripping away the trappings of womanhood help her achieve her goal, or are those trappings actually necessary for her to achieve it?

Characters

Poems offer some special challenges in terms of writing about characters, but in this poem there are some interesting options for this topic. As usual, the speaker of the poem is an important figure to consider as you write about character. And although it may seem as if there is little else to choose from in terms of characters, reading closely offers some ideas. Think about who is specifically mentioned in the poem by the speaker; who do you think the speaker is addressing in the work? Is it solely readers the speaker does not know, or does the poem seem aimed at a specific reader or specific readers? Look for clues in the poem about these questions as you consider an essay topic.

Sample Topics:

1. **The speaker:** Besides being the rider of the horse in this poem, who is the speaker?

What is the speaker's message in this poem? To whom is that message directed? What is the purpose of the speaker's narrative of this epic journey? Many critics see the speaker as androgynous, meaning not of either sex. How would you support this argument? How would you argue against it? What role does gender play in the speaker's journey? Is being a woman the reason the speaker must take this journey? What do you see as the defining characteristic(s) of the speaker? How do you think the speaker would define herself (or himself or itself)?

2. **Ariel:** Who is Ariel in this poem? What role does Ariel play in the ultimate fate of the speaker?

Especially in light of the fact that Plath took riding lessons, many see this poem as a horseback ride inspired by her own ride on her favorite horse, Ariel. How would you support this assertion? How might you argue against it? Judith Kroll argues that the name Ariel in this poem is used specifically by Plath, "alluding to a fiery sacrifice, purification, and transcendence. In Isaiah it is 'A cryptic name for Jerusalem.' The derivation of the name may be either 'lion (lioness) of God'" (181). How do the various associations with the name Ariel support or complicate the idea of Ariel as the steed that carries the speaker toward the burning cauldron at the end of the poem?

3. **The poet:** What are the dangers of reading this poem as strictly autobiographical?

Most likely because Plath's suicide is so famous, many readers are too inclined to assume all of Plath's works are fairly straightforward autobiography. However, as Christine Britzolakis notes, "Plath's experiments with voice and persona resist the tendency to read her poems as psychobiographical narrative" and her work actually "withholds from both poet and reader any secure identification" (108). What is gained by separating the life of the poet from the poem? How do readers gain a better understanding of the poem by looking past Plath's famous life story and concentrating on the tactics she uses as a poet?

History and Context

This poem was written just a few months before Plath's death, one of many poems she wrote in a short period of time while she was living in Devon after her separation from Ted Hughes. Frieda Hughes, Plath's daughter, writes in the foreword to *Ariel* that the way her mother put the collection together was "clearly geared to cover the ground from just before the breakup of the marriage to the resolution of a new life, with all the agonies and furies in between" (xii). Plath's anger over her husband's infidelity (his affair was the reason for the breakup of the marriage) likely influenced her first choice of a title for the collection, *The Rival*. "Her first idea was that the enemy suggested by 'the rival'— whether mother, sister, lover, or the self as double—was the dominant theme" of the poems in the collection (Wagner-Martin, *Biography* 227). There were at least two more choices for the title before Plath chose *Ariel;* this decision emphasizes the importance of this poem to her and to what she suspected would be her most successful body of work.

As you read this poem, it is also important to remember that during the late 1950s and early 1960s there were many politically and culturally important movements going on, including the cold war and the fight for civil rights and women's rights. Plath was concerned about these issues, and those preoccupations often show up in her work.

Sample Topics:

1. **Class and "cultural hierarchies":** Where do you see Plath challenging traditional notions of poetry as "high" culture in this poem?

   Christine Britzolakis argues that Plath's poems, including many in *Ariel*, call into question the idea of poetry and literature as "high" culture, an ideal closely held by readers and critics during the 1950s. Britzolakis argues these poems

"unsettle . . . cultural hierarchies" with their "visual spectacle" (115). How does this poem demonstrate Plath's use of
"visual spectacle" that might go against those traditional ideas
about poetry as high art? What might Plath be trying to do
by challenging those notions? How might her feelings about
mainstream poetry have been influenced by the success of her
husband, Ted Hughes, as a poet? What statements might she
be making about the place of men and the place of women as
artists in this cultural hierarchy?

2. **Battle of the sexes or joining of the sexes:** How does this poem
   illustrate a battle between the sexes? Conversely, how does it
   illustrate an abandonment of gender and a joining of male and
   female?

   Bundtzen writes that in this poem "the masculine and feminine components of Plath's personality join triumphantly in
   the figure of a divine androgyne" (254). How is the speaker
   empowered by her abandonment of her gender? Is her shedding of womanly features an act of revenge against a patriarchal system or an attempt at equality? How does this newly
   androgynous being emphasize the importance of creative
   energy above all else? Does one gender benefit more than the
   other from this new androgynous identity? What references
   in the work support a feminist reading of the poem as a commentary on unfair expectations for women?

3. **Science fiction:** How does this poem resemble a piece of science fiction? What conventions of science fiction do you see
   Plath working with, even playing with, in this poem?

   Science fiction as a genre was growing in popularity in the
   1950s and 1960s; while not often emphasized, in some of the
   short stories Plath wrote, she toyed with conventions of science fiction. What traits of science fiction do you see in this
   poem? How does employing elements of science fiction, such
   as surreal images and "visual spectacle," complement the idea

of the androgynous nature of the speaker? How might a science fiction feel in this poem help to illustrate a fear about the fate of the world in the era of technology like the hydrogen bomb? How might Plath be including ideas and visions of space travel into this poem? What might she be saying happens when we escape the bonds of Earth?

Philosophy and Ideas

As you reread the poem, think about what you see as the overall point of the work. You might want to think about some of the themes and images you see in the poem and consider what Plath might be saying about life in general. Plath was conscious of what was going on in the world around her and was often concerned about the fate of the world in light of the cold war and the aftermath of World War II. She also pondered her roles as a writer, as a mother, and as a wife and the difficulties of finding balance in all of those facets of her life.

When you consider possible topics for writing about Plath, thinking about what her work says about her views on life can be helpful. Basically, as you read this poem, consider what Plath is saying about issues and topics that would affect not only her but the culture and even the world around her. Thinking about the things Plath writes about in the bigger context of society in general can help you formulate a plan of attack for a paper or essay about her work.

Sample Topics:

1. **Objectification of women:** How is this poem an indictment of traditional roles for women? How does the ride that the speaker is on help her free herself from those roles?

   Wagner-Martin sees in this poem, and others in the collection, the figure of "a betrayed woman—sick, sexually abused, even dead" who "survives, and survives to mete out vengeance" (*Biography* 220). Think about whether you agree with this statement or not. If you do, how would you support the argument? Based on the poem, who or what is responsible for the betrayal of the woman? How does the woman in this poem demonstrate her vengeance for this betrayal?

Lynda Bundtzen argues that this is not "a poem directed toward vengeance or turning the tables on a male victimizer" (256). Obviously there are conflicting ways to read this poem; what do you think the message about women is in this poem?

2. **Impending apocalypse:** How does this poem illustrate Plath's fears about the cold war and the possibility that it would end in the annihilation of the world?

Plath's daughter, Frieda, calls this poem and others in the *Ariel* collection "poems of an otherworldly, menacing landscape," noting a "distinctive *Ariel* voice" (x) as a mark of the later poems her mother wrote. How do you see this "menacing landscape" illustrated in "Ariel"? How do you think the narrator of the poem feels about her fiery end? How do the biblical and religious references in the poem foster a feeling of the coming end of the world? Is the tone of the poem one of dread and fear for the end, or is it one of anticipation? Is the speaker in control of this end, or is it out of her control?

3. **Transcendence versus escape:** In this poem, is the speaker escaping her life and its trials, or is she transcending the everyday and achieving something divine?

First of all, it will be useful to consider the difference between escape and transcendence. The speaker jettisons parts of her self on this ride; is ridding herself of these things allowing her to escape her life or to rise above it? Is escape a necessary part of transcendence for the speaker? Which lines in the poem introduce readers to the things the speaker wishes to get away from or rise above? Why would the speaker wish to eliminate these things from her life? What exactly is the speaker flying into? Is the speaker hoping to save herself with this flight, or sacrifice herself? What is she saving herself from, or why is she sacrificing herself? What is the end result of her escape or transcendence?

4. **Empowerment:** From where does the speaker draw her power as she rides? What is the driving force behind this ride toward the sun?

Is Ariel, the horse, the true source of power in this poem? Does the speaker gain power from her own anger—the vengeance Martin-Wagner sees being doled out in the poem? Is she drawing on something specifically feminine within her—the "White Godiva" (19–20)? Kroll cites Robert Graves's notion of "Godiva actually being a white goddess of Love and Death, specially associated with the death of the sacred king" (182). How might this figure of the white goddess become part of the confessional nature of Plath's work, reflecting her own experiences with the breakup of her marriage? The speaker in this poem is constantly in motion, powered not only by the horse she rides but also by the momentum she gains by shedding "Dead hands, dead stringencies" (21). Is there a new, more powerful being created by the melding of the powers of the horse and rider?

Form and Genre

One great advantage that readers and writers have when reading "Ariel" is the access they have to Plath's own notes and revisions in the restored edition of the *Ariel* collection (see the bibliographic information at the end of this chapter). Because you can get a glimpse of Plath's writing process in the book, you can gain a better understanding of how she made decisions regarding word choice and format. Plath was a meticulous writer, so seeing some of the changes she made gives readers insight into those careful decisions she made when writing.

The style of Plath's poetry is usually considered confessional, a style of poetry in which poets include their own experiences and feelings in their poems. It is important to realize that simply because a writer includes his or her experiences in a piece of writing, it does not necessarily mean everything she or he writes is merely an account of her or his life. As you read the following ideas, keep in mind that Plath's goal was to write poems people would want to read, not just to write about her life.

Sample Topics:

1. **Revision:** How does the evidence of Plath's careful revision influence your reading of "Ariel?" Does it make the poem seem more or less autobiographical?

   In an early version of the work, the poem begins with the line "God's lioness also, how we grow" (Plath 175). How does moving the term *God's lioness* to its current location in the poem change the effect of this image? In this same version, the last two lines are "To the lover, the plunging / Hooves I am, that over and over" (175). What changes in the poem when the character of a lover is introduced? How does your thinking about "Ariel" change when the speaker references plunging hooves this way? Also notable in earlier versions of the poem are the lengths of the lines; it still had three-line stanzas, but the lines were longer. How is the motion of the poem changed by changing from seven stanzas (in the earlier versions) to the current eleven stanzas?

2. **Feminism in the style of Virginia Woolf:** How do you see this poem illustrating Virginia Woolf's theory about the need for "a room of one's own"?

   Virginia Woolf famously wrote that a woman needs "a room of one's own" in order to get writing done. How do you see Plath echoing this idea of a woman needing freedom in order to pursue her art in this poem? Is the speaker in essence seeking out this space, free from those expected womanly duties and decorum, for her creativity? According to Lynda Bundtzen, Plath was flattered when her work was compared to that of Woolf, but she also "feared cutting herself off from what she saw as the 'normal' experiences of womanhood—marriage, home, and most important, children" (21). How do you see the speaker trying to reconcile these two "sides" of her life—those normal experiences and the need to express herself through her art?

3. **Narrative style:** What is Plath trying to get readers to see with her careful attention to stanza breaks and punctuation?

What is emphasized in the poem when the phrasing is arranged as it is? What would change if the lines of the poem were arranged in a way that allowed for more complete sentences? One critic argues that in "Ariel" Plath is "replacing narrative sequence with a series of hallucinatory images, in language marked by a new rhythmic and colloquial freedom" (Britzolakis 107). How does this parade of images help to highlight the trajectory of the White Godiva on her horse? Do you see any kind of chronology in the poem? How does time get treated; is this something that happens instantly, or is the ride a long one that spans a lifetime?

Language, Symbols, and Imagery

As with many of Plath's poems, there are strong images and word choices in "Ariel." As you work through your ideas for an essay about this poem, remember to consider both the obvious choices and some that might not seem as obvious. While there are many words and images in this poem that might seem "easy" to write about, you also have to keep in mind that it is important for you to have an interest in what you choose for your writing project. Think about some of the symbolism or imagery you see in the poem that might not be as easily discussed and why you think it is important in this poem.

Another thing to keep in mind when writing about poetry, and especially imagery and language, is that it is not always spelled out for you. For instance, nowhere in "Ariel" does Plath actually use the words *horse* and *ride*, yet most experts who write about the poem agree that this is what Plath is writing about in the poem. What this should help demonstrate to you is that often you have to dig in and read between the lines when you are looking for images and symbolism in a poem. A writer often will not just hand over the entire meaning of a poem or novel to you—as a reader you have to do some work to understand what the writer is saying.

Sample Topics:

1. **Mythology:** Is the speaker in this poem a mythological figure, someone who does not exist but in legend, or is she an actual person undergoing a transformation of mythic proportions?

Mythological images and references show up a lot in this poem; the speaker refers to herself as "White Godiva." How is her horseback ride like that of Lady Godiva, who rode naked through the streets to protest the actions of her husband? The speaker's flight toward the sun also bears obvious similarities to the flight of Icarus, a figure from Greek mythology whose father made him a set of wings out of wax and feathers to help him escape from Crete. When Icarus flew too close to the sun, despite his father's warnings, the wax melted and Icarus died when he fell back to Earth. How does this flight toward the "red / Eye" (30–31) of the sun compare to the flight of Icarus? Will the speaker here be more successful?

2. **Rebirth:** What form will the speaker take after she flies into the sun? What will she become once she is reborn after this epic ride she has taken?

Wagner-Martin believes that in the *Ariel* collection, Plath "was telling a story, the story of her life as artist and married woman" and that, as in *The Bell Jar,* "she implied a healthy rebirth with her ending" (*Biography* 227). How do you see the ending of "Ariel" as an example of a "healthy rebirth"? Why is this symbolic death and rebirth even necessary? What does the speaker gain by being reborn? What words and images in the poem do you see as specifically addressing this idea of rebirth? How might you argue that the "Suicidal" (29) flight is not out of despair but out of hope? What is significant about the speaker taking matters into her own hands like this?

3. **Color:** How does color help readers follow the journey being taken by the speaker in this poem?

The poem begins in darkness and ends in the redness of the sun. As Britzolakis notes, "images of darkness, earth, blood, orality and the female body give way to those of light, transcendence and embodiment" (115). What is the significance of the colors that come up along the way? Darkness gives way to the "substanceless blue" (2); is this an initial leap that makes the rider airborne? What colors in the poem are associated with the earthly and which are associated with the heavenly? Why is the final image that of a "red / Eye" (30–31) instead of the "White Godiva" (19–20)? How does the progression of colors demonstrate a process of purification the speaker is undergoing?

4. **Metaphor:** Where are the metaphors in this poem? Which do you see as the most powerful or the most important?

Plath uses metaphors liberally in her work; in this poem they are especially important because the somewhat dis-jointed nature of the poem can make it difficult for readers to understand what's happening in the poem. How does Plath use metaphor to create an image of her life before she begins this ascent? What is the significance of the berries with their hooks? When the speaker says of herself, "And now I / Foam to wheat, a glitter of seas" (22–23), what transformation has taken place? When she claims that "I / Am the arrow" (26–27), is the speaker referring to herself as a weapon or as an arrow, straight and true, that will reach its target?

Compare and Contrast Essays

As you consider which works to use for a compare and contrast essay about "Ariel," there are many options that can be pursued successfully. Although this is a short poem, it is rich with elements that connect to other works. Of course, there are many reasons to compare and con-trast "Ariel" with other poems in the *Ariel* collection, and some ideas for doing that are offered below. However, there are also many benefits to looking at works by other writers. This poem especially offers writers several options for a compare and contrast essay because the name *Ariel* appears in so many different literary, religious, and mythological works and contexts. Be sure not to limit yourself to an essay related to the title character, though; there are many other options for compare and con-trast projects, as well.

Sample Topics:

1. **Ariel in the poem to Ariel in *The Tempest*:** How do these two characters compare? Do you see Plath playing off the Shakespearean character in this poem?

   Lynda Bundtzen argues that there is a clear connection between the title character of this poem and Shakespeare's Ariel because of the poem's "implicit statement about woman's creative energy." She goes on to say, "Shakespeare's Ariel is neither male nor female, so the divine activity of the poet is not a sexual prerogative. It is pure energy, both and neither male nor female, and belonging to no one" (Bundtzen 255). How do you see this comparison as valid, or even useful, in reading Plath's poem? What specific lines from the poem and examples from Shakespeare's play would you use to demonstrate the connection between the characters? Would you actually argue against a comparison like this? If so, what evidence would you use to support your argument?

2. **"Ariel" to "Lady Lazarus":** Many readers see "Ariel" as a poem full of optimism and power and "Lady Lazarus" as a poem illustrating the pain and darkness felt by Plath. How would you support this reading of the poems?

   These poems were basically written simultaneously; "Lady Lazarus" was in progress while Plath finished "Ariel" and completed just two days later. What words and images do you see in both of these poems? How are those words and images treated differently in each poem? As you reread the poems, look for examples of opposites like light and dark, life and death, male and female, private and public—how do you see opposites in these two poems? What do you think they might symbolize? How do you think they might reflect Plath's own experience? Do you think that Ariel and Lady Lazarus are the same voice speaking in two different poems?

3. **"Ariel" to the work of Emily Dickinson:** Where do you see the influence of Emily Dickinson in this poem? What is different

about this poem from others by Plath that helps demonstrate this influence?

Annas says of this poem, "it is one of the more compact and abstract, obscure and Emily Dickinson–like poems in [*Ariel*]" (127). What is it about this poem that mirrors Dickinson's work? Do you think Plath is paying homage to Dickinson? Attempting to continue a conversation Dickinson started? Dickinson's poems were written a century before Plath wrote "Ariel"; choose one or two of Dickinson's poems (Dickinson's poem number 593 from 1862 would be a good option). What do you see as common ground between the works? Do you see themes that are present in both poems? What effect does the century between the two works have?

4. **Ariel in the poem and Ariel in the Bible:** How is the figure of Ariel in this poem a divine one? How does the flight of Ariel in this poem become a religious experience?

Judith Kroll argues that Plath purposefully incorporates the name Ariel because of its religious connotations, including the line in the poem in which the speaker calls herself "God's lioness" (4). How is the figure in this poem fighting for God? Kroll also points to the images of fiery sacrifices as allusion to holocaust. Why would the speaker offer herself up for sacrifice? How does the shedding of parts of her self reflect religious sacrifice? What does the speaker believe will happen to her when she finally achieves purification? Is the speaker trying to become one with God, or with something else? Why is fire in the poem associated with salvation rather than with the more familiar association with hell?

Bibliography and Online Resources for "Ariel"

Annas, Pamela. *A Disturbance in Mirrors: The Poetry of Sylvia Plath*. New York: Greenwood P, 1988. Print.

Brennan, Claire, ed. *The Poetry of Sylvia Plath*. New York: Columbia UP, 1999. Print. Columbia Critical Guides.

Britzolakis, Christine. *"Ariel* and other poems." *The Cambridge Companion to Sylvia Plath.* Jo Gill, ed. Cambridge: Cambridge UP, 2006. Print. 107–23.

Bundtzen, Lynda. *Plath's Incarnations: Woman and the Creative Process.* Ann Arbor, MI: U of Michigan P, 1983. Print.

Hughes, Frieda. Forward. Sylvia Plath. *Ariel: The Restored Edition.* London: Faber and Faber, 2004. Print. ix–xvii.

Kroll, Judith. *Chapters in a Mythology: The Poetry of Sylvia Plath.* New York: Harper and Row, 1976. Print.

Plath, Sylvia. *Ariel: The Restored Edition.* London: Faber and Faber, 2004.

Wagner-Martin, Linda. *Sylvia Plath: A Biography.* New York: Simon and Schuster, 1987. Print.

———. *Sylvia Plath: A Literary Life.* Hampshire, England:Macmillan P, 1999. Print.

"DADDY"

READING TO WRITE

Of all the poems Sylvia Plath wrote, it is arguably this one that produces the most reaction and even controversy. "Daddy" was one of the poems Plath wrote in 1962, shortly before her death, and included in the *Ariel* collection. While the poem has a number of undeniably autobiographical notes to it, there are many critics who argue that Plath is tackling much larger issues with this poem. Many readers, especially those inexperienced with literary analysis or unaccustomed to reading for deeper meaning, take the poem at what might be called face value—reading it as Plath's expression of anger at a tyrannical father and including her resentment at a cheating husband as she does. However, by examining the poem more deeply, some of those other themes and ideas start to become more obvious. As Connie Ann Kirk points out, "Daddy" is often misunderstood:

> The poem is terrifying to many readers, some of whom do not understand its references to the father as a German Nazi. Sylvia was combining images of her father, her husband, and perhaps other male figures at whom she had been very angry over a lifetime together in the image of the father in the poem. (119)

Otto Plath died when his daughter Sylvia was eight. What began as symptoms of fatigue and weight loss grew more serious, but the professor refused to go in for medical treatment, most likely because he thought he might be terminally ill. When one of his legs became discolored, Sylvia's mother insisted he go in for treatment. The problem turned out to be related to diabetes, an ailment that could have been treated easily had he gone in earlier. After having the leg amputated, he refused to return home and ultimately died of an embolism in his lung (Stevenson 9–10). After his death, Plath's mother made "what may have been a crucial mistake in not taking the children to their father's funeral and in not encouraging them to outwardly grieve" (Kirk 46).

The loss of her father naturally dogged Plath throughout her own life. As Edward Butscher notes:

> even the most casual reading of [Plath's] poetry demonstrates . . . the central obsession from the beginning to the end of her life and career was her father. . . . His life and, more importantly, his death nine days after her eighth birthday left an imprint upon her imagination that time did not erase or soften. (3)

Because of this, it is no surprise that Otto Plath becomes a prominent figure in much of Plath's poetry. As Kirk points out, though, sometimes the emotions readers see expressed in the poem can seem frightening.

As you read the poem, it could be useful to think not solely about the literal meanings and images Plath writes, but instead to think of metaphors and references she makes. An example can be seen in these two stanzas:

> It stuck in a barb wire snare.
> Ich, ich, ich, ich,
> I could hardly speak.
> I thought every German was you.
> And the language was obscene
> An engine, an engine
> Chuffing me off like a Jew.
> A Jew to Dachau, Auschwitz, Belsen.
> I began to talk like a Jew.
> I think I may well be a Jew. (Plath 26–35)

There have been many critics throughout the years who have voiced strong objections to Plath using Holocaust imagery in this poem and likening herself to a Jew. As Jacqueline Rose points out, in most of the outraged criticisms of this poem, "the key concept appears to be meta-phor—either Plath trivializes the Holocaust . . . or she aggrandizes her experience by stealing the historical event" (206). Rose goes on to say that the most important question to ask might not be whether Plath has a right to use Holocaust images this way, "but what the presence of the Holocaust in her poetry unleashes, or obliges us to focus" on as we read it (207).

Bearing this in mind, then, you should consider this question: What does Plath's inclusion of these direct references to Jews being "chuffed" off to concentration camps make readers think about? If you focus on the idea of Plath forcing readers to remember horrifying injustices rather than literally claiming to be a Jew, you open up an avenue to explore possible topics for papers and essays. Knowing that Plath was a politically engaged young woman helps to illustrate that point even further. In her journal, she writes of her consideration of a "complicated guilt system" related to Germans living in America after the actions of the Nazis in World War II (Kukil 453). World War II and its aftermath continued to haunt Plath, which shows up often, as it does in this poem.

One way to read Plath's inclusion of these startling images and comparisons is to see the tactic as a way to make readers understand their distance from the actuality of the Holocaust and possibly even their own involvement in it. Because she was so moved by the events of World War II and so concerned about the politics of both the United States and Great Britain during the cold war of the 1950s and 1960s, this poem could be read as a kind of reminder to readers who were already nearly a generation removed from the Holocaust. In the poem, she is asserting her independence from this dark figure of "Daddy" who has kept her under his foot for her entire life. Rather than an indictment against her father, this work can be seen as an indictment against the patriarchal society in which she lives. This patriarchal system not only keeps her under its foot because she is a woman, but it also threatens to "chuff" off anyone who does not abide by its policies, man or woman.

Author Langdon Hammer writes of Plath's fascination and horror with war. Even as a child, her work at school on a report about World War I showed her belief that "she is a part of the history she reports on, and that it is part of her" (147). With that in mind, consider what Plath might be saying to those who see the war as a thing of the past, comfortable to leave it in the past. Although it had been ended, the lasting effects of the war, including the efforts to exterminate the Jews, were still being felt. As you reread the work, look for statements Plath might be making about keeping this monstrous part of human history alive in readers' minds. While in school, Plath corresponded with a West German student, noting that she had not had firsthand experience with war while he had and that her distance from that history bothered her (Hammer 151–52). Thus, although she is, at least in part, addressing personal issues in this poem, using the framework of the Holocaust to express them suggests she is sending a message to readers about how integral these events still are in people's lives and how important it is that they not be cast aside.

Plath herself introduced this poem for a BBC broadcast by saying the speaker was "a girl with an Electra complex. Her father died when she thought he was God. Her case is complicated by the fact that her father was also a Nazi and her mother possibly part Jewish. In the daughter the two strains marry and paralyze each other—she has to act out the awful little allegory once over before she is free of it" (194). Once again, Plath draws attention to the fact that the speaker's voice in the poem, while containing elements of her own, has clearly been created as a tool for delivering the message of the work. As you reread the poem and decide on a topic for an essay, focus on what you see as the message, or messages, Plath is sending readers through "Daddy."

TOPICS AND STRATEGIES

Perhaps especially because this poem is so fraught with controversy, there are myriad opportunities for you to find a strong and resonant essay topic. The rich and troubling images Plath provides in the poem are worthy of discussion, as are the historical elements of the work. The following ideas for paper topics are clearly not a comprehensive list, but they may offer you some tools for finding a topic that suits your reading of the poem. This is one of Plath's most hotly debated works, so there is also no lack of reading material related to this poem that could help you with a research project. Remember to think about the different approaches you can take based on the different ways of reading this poem; there is no doubt this can be a difficult poem to write about, but if you make some decisions about how you are going to read the poem, that can help you get started on a paper or essay.

Themes

There are some themes that are quick to emerge when you first read "Daddy." Those can be helpful when you start writing a paper, but sometimes thinking about themes that do not seem quite as obvious can offer you an even better opportunity to include your own insight in a paper or essay. The themes listed below are certainly not the only ones that a writer can tackle in a paper. Rather, think of these ideas as icebreakers—introductions to some ideas and questions you might ask yourself as you get started on an essay. These themes represent some things Plath wrestled with in other works, as well. As has been said throughout this book, as you decide on a topic for an essay, it is important to read "Daddy" not merely as a sign that Plath was depressed but as a piece that was purposefully written by Plath to spark reaction in readers.

Sample Topics:

1. **Loss:** What different kinds of loss is Plath exploring in this poem?

   Obviously Plath is working through her feelings about the death of her father in this poem. Reportedly, she once told a friend, "Otto had not wanted a child but, after seeing her, changed his mind and loved her very much. True or not, it was part of the myth of childhood that Sylvia would find essential to maintain" (Butscher 8). What is she saying in this poem that she has lost because of the death of her father? She also references the breakup of her marriage to Ted Hughes. How does that loss compound the loss of her father? What statements might she be making about the loss of the Jews in World War II?

2. **War:** What statements is Plath making about war in this poem?

   The references to the Jews and the Holocaust in this poem clearly make readers think of World War II. Why is she using those references in a poem that is ostensibly about her father? What is she saying about the Holocaust? Is she making comparisons between actual holocaust and emotional holocaust? As Langdon Hammer writes, "In 'Daddy' and other poems from later in her career, Plath brought the historical violence of World War II and the Holocaust into troubling, unexpected conjunction with the domestic relationships between father and daughter and husband and wife" (147). What is she saying about those relationships? Is she asserting that men and women are at war with each other? Who is victorious in that war?

3. **Family relationships:** How does the speaker characterize her relationship with her father in this poem?

   Although the speaker's mother is not a named character in the poem, what role does she play in what has transpired between the speaker and her father? Lynda Bundtzen argues that this poem can be seen as an allegory

   > about the way in which the father-daughter relationship domi-
   > nates the female psyche in our culture. Father and daughter
   > are exaggerated figures of authority and obedience—exagger-
   > ated, not in order to magnify Otto Plath's villainy or Sylvia
   > Plath's personal suffering, but in order to explore the tragic
   > glory of father worship. (159)

   How does reading the poem as an allegory like this complement or conflict with the inclusion of the "vampire who said
   he was you" (72) to whom she said, "I do, I do?" (67).

4. **Control.** Who is in control in this poem? Is the speaker's daddy still in control, or has she taken it away from him?

   Al Alvarez, a friend of Sylvia Plath's, writes that one of the most important parts of Plath's upbringing was the fact that both of her parents were "of German stock and were German-speaking, academic and intellectual" (188). Could the references to German brutality in this poem be read as an expression of Plath's desire to rebel against the kind of lives they had? How could you read the poem as a statement about rebellion and taking control of one's own destiny? How does the death of the speaker's father in the poem actually serve to give him more control over her rather than less? How could these statements be used to decide what Plath might be saying about governmental or institutional control?

Characters

The most obvious characters in this poem are the speaker and Daddy. However, there are many readers who argue that the mother plays an important, if not completely obvious, role in this poem, as well. Her friend Al Alvarez thought that for Plath this poem was an expression of "the struggle in her between fantasy Nazi father and a Jewish mother. But perhaps it was also a fantasy of containing in herself her own dead father" (211). Another character who appears in the poem is the speaker's husband, whom she sees as another version of her daddy. Although in poetry it can seem more difficult to discern characters and write about them than in longer works of fiction like novels and even short stories, these ideas might help you decide on a way you can address the element of character in this poem and formulate a plan for an essay or other project.

Sample Topics:

1. **Daddy:** What is the speaker accusing her Daddy of doing to her? What was his biggest sin?

   Is she blaming him for his own death? Is she blaming him for her attempt to end her own life? Why does she characterize him as a "Panzer-man" and liken him so clearly to a Nazi? How has his death imprisoned her like the Nazis imprisoned the Jews? It was only after Otto Plath stubbed his toe, which led to his foot and leg becoming terribly discolored, that he agreed he needed medical attention (Stevenson 9–10). That, in part, explains the image of the "one gray toe / Big as a Frisco seal" in lines 9 and 10 of the poem, but why would Plath include that image? Is she suggesting her father shared some blame in his own death? Why switch in the last two stanzas of the poem to likening him to a vampire? How has he sucked the life out of her?

2. **The speaker:** Is this poem a cathartic exercise for the speaker? Do you believe she achieves catharsis by the end of the poem?

Plath had a clear idea of who the speaker is in this poem. Ronald Hayman notes, "while the speaker is partly a character . . . as in so many of Sylvia Plath's poems, the tone is so abrasively confessional that we can't be entirely deceived. . . . The girl with the Nazi father is a persona, but the mask is designed to become transparent" (31). Where in the poem do you see Plath creating a character rather than speaking specifically of herself? Has the speaker come to grips with the death of her father? Do you think Plath is saying she has or has not? Why does the speaker include her husband in the poem? Did she choose the man because he reminded her of her daddy, or is it her fate to have this relationship with any man? What do you think the speaker is saying about her father and her husband? What message do you think Plath wants to send to readers with this poem?

3. **The mother:** How is the mother of the speaker present in this poem?

Although there is no mother directly addressed in this poem, since the speaker is discussing her father, she obviously also had a mother. What is that mother's role in the relationship between Daddy and the speaker? Does she act as an intercessor, or is she a hindrance? Is the mother also a victim of this blackhearted figure? In the line "Every woman adores a Fascist" (48), is the speaker referring to herself or to her mother? Find specific lines or words you think signal the presence of the mother in this poem and decide how they show the mother working with or against the father's presence. Would you argue that the speaker has sympathy for her mother or not?

4. **The husband:** What role does the husband play in this poem? Why does the speaker include him in this diatribe about her father?

Whose transgression was worse to the speaker—her father's or her husband's? Do you believe the rush of emotion in this poem is primarily directed at the speaker's father or at her husband? When the speaker says, "I made a model of you" (64), does the speaker blame her father for making her search out men who are like him because of his death? As you read the poem again, consider whether you believe the desertion of the husband was necessary to spark the emotions needed for the speaker to finally declare, "I'm through" (80). If she is, indeed, through with her daddy, does that mean she is also through with her husband?

History and Context

This poem was written as part of the collection ultimately titled *Ariel*— the poems Plath wrote just months before her death, and the work many readers and critics consider her best. She and her husband, Ted Hughes, had just separated, and she had decided to pursue a divorce. Plath was still living in Devon with her two children when she wrote "Daddy" but would soon decide to move back to London. At this point, Plath knew she was writing well, claiming in a letter to her mother that she was happy with her work and felt she had achieved genius, realizing at the time she was writing poetry that would make her famous (Stevenson 267).

In the early 1960s, much of the world (including England) was still recovering from the devastation of World War II, and the cold war pitted the United States and its allies against Russia and its allies. Plath was terrified by the idea of another war and in many of her letters and journals writes of the horror she felt when hearing stories about Nagasaki, writing, "God save us from doing that again" (Kukil 46). As in much of her work, these fears come through in the text of "Daddy."

Sample Topics:

1. **War:** How can this poem be read as an indictment of the cold war and even war in general?

   Jacqueline Rose notes that in many of Plath's short stories, "the personal wrong the narrator suffers, the collapse of justice, is given its fullest meaning in the context of the war" (201). Do you see this happening in "Daddy"? How is the story of the speaker's anger against her father affected by combining it with images of the Holocaust? If you read this poem as a representation of the speaker at war with the ghost of her father, how does that support an argument that Plath was urging readers not to forget the tragedies of World War II? How does Plath illustrate the idea of a post–World War II world at war with the ghost of the Holocaust in this poem? What might Plath be saying about facing the truth of what the Nazis did and stopping those atrocities from being repeated?

2. **Gender issues:** How is Plath addressing inequities in the treatment of women in this poem? What is she saying about the power of men versus the power of women?

   Several critics argue that Plath is making strong statements about a patriarchal structure's treatment of women in this poem. The use of Nazi/Jew becomes a way to talk about the subjugation of women by men; "the representation of the father as Nazi would reveal something about the violence of patriarchy" (Rose 235). How do you see these sorts of feminist statements being made in this poem? How does that change the way the Holocaust imagery is being used in the poem? How do you see Plath's own situation, the poet-wife of a more successful poet, and daughter of a reportedly unhappy housewife, contributing to a feminist reading of this poem? Rose also notes there are problems with reading the poem from this standpoint; what problems do you think a reader wishing to find a feminist message in this poem might find? What details from the poem support a feminist reading? When Plath writes, "Every woman adores a Fascist" (48), what might she be saying about women's roles in the subjugation of women?

3. **The past's role in the present:** Plath's personal history is obviously a crucial part of this poem. Why does she combine her childhood with comparisons to being Jewish in this poem?

Plath's references are purposeful in "Daddy"; Lynda Bundtzen agrees, noting, "There is nothing unconscious about the poem, instead it seems to force into consciousness the child's dread and love for the father, so that those feelings may be resolved" (93). What might Plath be saying about how the past treatment of the Jews still affects people, even though the war is over? How can this poem be read as an illustration of how the atrocities of the past must be completely put to rest before the world can move on? Plath was concerned about the prospect of another war—how does that concern manifest itself in this poem?

Philosophy and Ideas

Although this book argues against reading Plath's works as solely autobiographical and as indicators of her impending suicide, there is no doubt that many of the poems in the *Ariel* collection are emotionally charged and show her wrestling with raw emotions. At the time she wrote "Daddy," she had found out her husband, Ted Hughes, was having an affair with a mutual friend of theirs, Assia Wevill. She had seen some of her work published and had received good news about publication of *The Bell Jar*, but she was still not achieving the kind of professional recognition for her writing that she craved.

Undoubtedly, these personal trials played a major role in her writing at this time, but there, as always, are larger issues being addressed in the writing, as well. As you decide on a topic for an essay about Plath and/or her work, consider how her personal troubles might have prodded her to write about those issues. What might she have been saying to the readers she hoped to reach about things that are common to all people? As you abandon the tortured writer stereotype and consider Plath as a writer with a purpose for her work, you will find that there are many excellent topics that can be used in your writing. The following are some ideas to get you started.

Sample Topics:

1. **Catharsis:** Is the speaker making a conscious effort to put an end to her grieving? Does she realize, or believe, that working through this "awful little allegory" will offer her relief from her suffering?

   Many readers of this poem agree with this assertion by Connie Ann Kirk: "When the speaker says she is through with Daddy at the end of the poem, Sylvia seems to have worked her way through, and become done with, all of these male-dominating forces that had frustrated her for so long" (119). How would you either support or argue against that statement? Do you think Plath is saying it is possible for the speaker to achieve catharsis, or will she be working through her grief forever? In bringing in the references to the Holocaust, what might Plath be saying about recovering from the grief caused by the horrors of World War II? By saying she might be "a bit of a Jew" (40), how might she be suggesting that there is no way to truly recover from wrongs such as those committed by the Nazis?

2. **Abandonment and detachment:** In a journal entry from 1958, Plath writes, "I hated men because they didn't stay around and love me like a father" (Kukil 431). How do you see this poem as a reflection of those feelings?

   How does her father's abandonment compare to the abandonment of her husband in this poem? Is either more hurtful than the other? Does the speaker see the men working together against her, or are they just two separately hurtful entities? By incorporating Holocaust references, Plath is inferring some parallels. The speaker was abandoned by her father in this poem; who is she saying abandoned the Jews? Ann Keniston notes the outrage many readers have about Plath's use of Holocaust imagery in this and other poems, but she argues, "Plath's speakers do not in fact pretend to be witnesses or survivors of the Holocaust. Rather than revealing proximity and immediacy, they occupy a position of distance and belatedness" (140). How does Keniston's idea of "distance and belatedness" apply to readers of this poem? How might Plath be pointing out her own detachment from the plight of the Jews, even by announcing she "might be a bit of a Jew"?

3. **Social responsibility:** How is Plath pointing out apathy about social issues in this poem?

Sylvia Plath was a pacifist; she developed those views "which were strongly associated with her father under her high school English teacher . . . who emphasized social responsibility and made writing a means to advance it" (Hammer 151). How does this poem serve as a warning to readers about becoming apathetic about issues like war and women's rights? In one journal, she writes, "Freedom is not of use to those who do not know how to employ it" (Kukil 46). By bringing up the Holocaust in this poem, what might she be trying to make readers think about in terms of their own freedoms? For a school project, she and a classmate pointed out the number of enemy civilians America had killed in World War II, arguing against the wisdom of the cold war (Hammer 151). How does her incorporation of the internment of the Jews into this poem highlight her feelings about the apathy of the general public?

Form and Genre

This poem is commonly referred to as an allegory, even by Plath herself. An allegory uses fictional figures or situations to symbolize truth; allegories are often used as a way to explore truths about human nature. If you think of this as you reread the poem, it might open up new avenues for you to explore for essay topics. Another important thing to keep in mind about this poem is that it is considered a prime example of the confessional poetry genre. Confessional poetry commonly contains personal information about a poet's life, and the 1950s and 1960s is seen as a major time of development for the genre. Plath admired poets like Robert Lowell and Anne Sexton, who are widely considered Plath's major peers in the confessional movement. As you read though the following ideas, consider how you would support your own reading of the poem. How might you categorize the poem?

Sample Topics:

1. **Allegory:** What truths about human existence are being explored in the allegory of this poem?

   For a BBC broadcast, Plath discussed this poem before reading it, saying of the speaker in this poem, "'She has to act out the awful little allegory once over before she is free of it'" (Alvarez 211). Why is using the Holocaust an effective vehicle for acting out this particular allegory? What does the inclusion of war references add to the statement about truth being made in this allegory? Many writers employ a story-within-a-story model to make points about human nature. How might this poem be read as an allegory within an allegory? Does Plath create an allegory for her speaker that she, herself, must act out? Is the act of writing the way Plath acts out her own allegory?

2. **The importance of reading work aloud:** Read this poem out loud to yourself. How does speaking it change your understanding of the poem?

   Al Alvarez recalls when Plath stopped in to read him some of her poems, including "Daddy." He writes, "Her voice . . . was hot and full of venom. . . . I was appalled. At first hearing, the things seemed to be not so much poetry as assault and battery" (195). The Internet offers many links to recordings of Plath reading "Daddy." Listen to one and consider Alvarez's comments. How does Plath's verbal inflection reinforce specific images in the poem? Which words are the most emphasized in a recitation of the poem? How do even seemingly minor elements, like commas and periods, take on more meaning when you hear them used in a reading of the poem? How does hearing Plath read this poem aloud influence how you might read other of her works?

3. **Rhythm:** How does the rhythm of this poem emphasize the speaker's emotions? How does it help to explain those emotions?

How does the rhythm of this poem reflect the speaker's development from child to adult? Because the action of the poem begins when the speaker is a child, Bundtzen believes Plath "evokes the child's world with her own versions of Mother Goose rhymes" (think of the old woman who lived in a shoe) in the first stanzas of the poem, but then, those rhythms "gradually build to a goose step march as the mourning process turns inward" (93). What images or words seem particularly useful to you in demonstrating this change from outward mourning to inward mourning? What effect does it have on readers of the poem when Plath incorporates a marching-style cadence into the poem? How does the repetition of certain words affect their meaning?

Language, Symbols, and Imagery

Arguably the Holocaust imagery in this poem gets the most notice and discussion from readers. Plath obviously intended for that imagery to influence readers, and it seems unlikely that she did not intend for readers to think about war and the attempted obliteration of an entire group of people. As has been brought up multiple times in this chapter, countless readers and critics were upset by her use of Holocaust imagery and thought it incredibly unfair of her to speak of being a Jew, especially since she was not Jewish. Keniston's point about Plath making a point of showing her speaker as in many ways detached from the Holocaust is a valid one to consider while reading this poem. There is much to write about regarding Holocaust imagery in this poem, but taking the road less traveled may actually prove a more manageable task when choosing a topic for an essay or other project.

The allegorical nature of this poem also offers rich opportunities for writing. As you consider a topic, you might find it valuable to do some research about the war so you can read the poem at an even deeper level.

It could also prove useful to find out more about Plath's father, Otto. Edward Butscher notes: "those who knew Otto Plath intimately agreed that he was nothing like the Prussian tyrant later projected by his daughter's writing; but in varying degrees they also felt that there was a certain rigidity about him, a stiffness in his behavior and attitudes, which became more pronounced as he grew older" (7). The following ideas are by no means a complete list of the images and symbols that can be found in this poem, but they should give you some ideas to get you started as you think about what you want to write.

Sample Topics:

1. **Germanness and the Holocaust:** What does the Holocaust imagery communicate to a modern reader? How might a reader today see it differently than one who read the poem when it was first published?

   Plath is playing on stereotypes of Germans in this poem, most obviously with the Holocaust references, but also in the incorporation of German words and images. Which stereotypes is she capitalizing on? How is she able to use them to heighten the image of him as a villain? Both parents spoke German; her mother even taught it. They were also both German, so what might she be saying about a kind of collective responsibility for what happened during the Holocaust? What is being a Jew symbolic of, especially for a woman from a German background? Another possible reason for relating Germans to villainy could be chalked up to the fact that her husband's mistress, Assia Wevill, was German. How might she be using this personal experience as a warning (with a political undertone) for readers about trusting those who seem to be innocent but can actually do great harm to us? Is Plath expressing a sort of national guilt for the Holocaust because of her German background? What might she be saying about which side it is better to be part of—the tyrannical or the tyrannized?

2. **Survival:** Is the speaker in this poem a victim or a survivor? Or both?

How does being a Jew make a difference in her story? According to Alvarez, Plath had a "queer conception of the adult as survivor, an imaginary Jew from the concentration camps of the mind" (197). When the speaker says she might be a Jew, does she mean a Jew who has survived the Holocaust? Is she likening herself to a group that was basically helpless when it was attacked, as were the Jews? What might she be saying about those who stood by and did nothing until it was too late for many who belonged to that group? What is the significance of surviving the vampire who drank her blood for so long? Has the speaker's experience with the Panzer man made her stronger and thus able to vanquish both him and the vampire? Or has it sentenced her to a lifetime of victimization by both of them, no matter how hard she fights?

3. **Death.** Why is it necessary for the speaker to kill her father in order to be through with him, especially since he is already dead?

There are many mentions of death in this poem, including in the second stanza when the speaker says, "I have had to kill you. / You died before I had time—" (6–7). What does she mean by this? Referring back to Plath's own words about the poem, she says the girl's father died when she thought he was still God. Did she need time to realize he was only human? The speaker also notes that she attempted suicide so she could get "back, back, back to you" (59), but she was unsuccessful. What is the speaker saying about death when she talks about being like a Jew being sent off to a concentration camp? Has her father actually sentenced her to death by his own dying? By likening him, and her husband, to vampires, is the speaker saying they will never actually die?

4. **Hope:** How might you argue that the speaker in this poem has hope for her future now that she is through with Daddy?

Although this poem is filled with dark images and references to horrifying events, many readers also see a message of hope

and even rebirth. How might Plath actually be making a statement about hopefulness for the speaker's future? The poem
ends with the words "I'm through" (80); does this signal a new
start for her? By killing her father and the vampire that was
her husband, has she created a new existence for herself? How
might the references to being a Jew be read as a sign that she
has been liberated, despite the efforts by the Panzer man and
the vampire to exterminate her?

Compare and Contrast

There are many choices that can be made to formulate a successful compare and contrast paper about this poem. There are two comparisons
that are often made by critics who write about Plath's work: to the poem
"Medusa," which is about Plath's relationship with her mother, and to
"Lady Lazarus," in which Plath delves into her own attempts at dying.
There are, however, many advantages to comparing Plath's writing to
that of other writers as well. The following list of ideas is meant as a
starting point for you; there are many options in Plath's collections that
would serve you well in a paper of this type.

There are also innumerable authors who have been inspired by Plath's
writing whose works would prove a fertile ground for comparison and
contrast. As you decide upon a piece to use for this type of essay, one
thing to remember is that you need to be able to analyze each piece similarly. For instance, rather than comparing a poem to an entire novel, you
might want to choose a small section of the novel to use in your essay.
Use the following ideas as tools with which you can develop your own
ideas for an essay.

Sample Topics:

1. **"Daddy" and "Medusa"**: How would you describe the ways
   the two poems illustrate the different feelings Plath has for her
   parents?

   These poems were written just days apart. While Plath made
   it plain she was writing about her father in "Daddy," it is quite
   likely her mother would recognize herself in "Medusa," as well.
   Not only is Medusa a famous figure from mythology, but it is

also a species of jellyfish, called the aurela—too similar to Aurelia for her mother to ignore (Hayman 181). Lynda Bundtzen
argues that "Daddy" is a successful and powerful allegory, but
"Medusa" falls short; she claims, "the poem remains incoher-
ent, inadequate to the feelings toward her mother that Plath is
trying to express," whereas in "Daddy" she claims, "Plath knew
what she wanted to say before she says it" (106). How would
you characterize the differences between the two poems? Is she
sending the same message about her parents? Which do you
think she blames more for the situation she is in?

2. **Anne Sexton's "My Friend, My Friend":** What do the recurring lines about becoming a Jew or being a Jew signify in these
   poems?

Sexton's poem was written in 1959, and there are varying
degrees of support for the idea that this poem at least in part
inspired "Daddy." Plath and Sexton knew each other from
school, and Plath writes admiringly of Sexton in her journal:
"She has none of my clenches and an ease of phrase, and an
honesty" (Kukil 477). How would you either support or discount the idea that Plath was influenced by Sexton when she
wrote this work? How does each of the poets characterize
being Jewish—is it a positive or negative state? What might
these poems be saying about women and women's roles? About
the role of religion in the life of the poem's speaker?

3. *Birthday Letters* **by Ted Hughes:** How does what Ted Hughes
   writes about the end of his marriage to Sylvia Plath work with,
   or against, her own writing about it?

In his book *Birthday Letters*, Ted Hughes finally writes about
his relationship with Sylvia Plath. Choose a work from that
book and compare it to "Daddy." How did Hughes talk about
the breakup of his marriage to Plath in his poetry? What was
going on for him at this time? When you read his work, do you
see it as defending his actions? Apologizing to Plath? Many

avid fans blame Hughes for Plath's suicide, even going so far as to scrape the name Hughes off of her gravestone. Does Hughes seem to have an understanding of that anger toward him? Even according to Plath, Hughes played a significant role in her writing; do you see any of Plath's influence in Hughes's work?

4. **"Daddy" and "Lady Lazarus":** "Lady Lazarus" was written shortly after "Daddy" and also features images of the Holocaust. How do you see those images being used in each of the poems to make a statement about death? How are they different?

These poems are almost always mentioned together in a discussion of Plath's works. In the first, "Daddy," she deals with her father's death, and in "Lady Lazarus," written just weeks later, she's talking about her own. How would you describe the difference in tone in each of the poems? What do you think the common messages communicated in the two poems might be? What is the significance of the violence in the killing of "Daddy" and the matter-of-fact voice discussing killing herself in "Lady Lazarus"? How does the character of Herr Doktor in the latter poem relate to Daddy in the earlier one? Is he the same man, or is he another figure? How is rebirth represented in each of these poems?

Bibliography and Online Resources for "Daddy"

Alvarez, A. "Sylvia Plath: A Memoir." *Ariel Ascending: Writings About Sylvia Plath.* Ed. Paul Alexander. New York: Harper and Row, 1985.

Bundtzen, Lynda. *Plath's Incarnations: Woman and the Creative Process.* Ann Arbor, MI: U of Michigan P, 1983. Print.

Butscher, Edward. *Sylvia Plath: Method and Madness.* New York: Seabury P, 1976. Print.

Hammer, Langdon. "Plath at War." *Eye Rhymes: Sylvia Plath's Art of the Visual.* Kathleen Connors and Sally Bayley, Eds. Oxford: Oxford U P, 2007. 145–57. Print.

Hayman, Ronald. *The Death and Life of Sylvia Plath.* New York: Carol, 1991.

Keniston, Ann. "The Holocaust Again: Sylvia Plath, Belatedness, and the Limits of Lyric Figure." *The Unraveling Archive: Essays on Sylvia Plath.* Anita Helle, ed. Ann Arbor: U of Michigan P, 2007. 139–57. Print.

Kirk, Connie Ann. *Sylvia Plath: A Biography.* Amherst, NY: Prometheus, 2009. Print.

Kukil, Karen V. *The Unabridged Journals of Sylvia Plath.* New York: Anchor Books, 2001. Print.

Rose, Jacqueline. *The Haunting of Sylvia Plath.* Cambridge, MA: Harvard U P, 1992. Print.

Plath, Sylvia. "Daddy." *Ariel: The Restored Edition.* London: Faber and Faber, 2004. Print.

Stevenson, Anne. *Bitter Fame: A Life of Sylvia Plath.* Boston: Houghton Mifflin, 1989. Print.

"LADY LAZARUS"

READING TO WRITE

"Lady Lazarus" is one of Plath's most famous and widely discussed poems. It is commonly paired with "Daddy" in literary discussions, not only because they were written at about the same time, October of 1962, but also because of the startling and bold images and sentiments in the poems. Readers, often almost unconsciously, read Plath's work in terms of her suicide. Every work, then, becomes a kind of indicator or precursor to her taking her own life. Plath's daughter, Frieda Hughes, gets frustrated by this approach to reading her mother's work: "I saw poems such as 'Lady Lazarus' and 'Daddy' dissected over and over, the moment that my mother wrote them being applied to her whole life, to her whole person, as if they were the total sum of her experience" (xiv). Lynda Bundtzen, a Plath biographer and professor of English, agrees, noting that "Such commentary encourages the reader to believe that she or he can comprehend the full scope of Plath's imagination on the basis of her final work, and even then, apparently, from a handful of these poems" (160–61).

To completely set aside Plath's personal history when reading "Lady Lazarus" is almost impossible, though. However, one thing to keep in mind as you read it is the way that Plath connects her own experiences to larger issues and how important it is to see how she is working with things from her own life and putting them into a larger context. She is also quite adept at making references to things and events that do not seem obvious at first—most likely because of that tendency to basically "settle" on the idea that everything she wrote was about her own life and that is that. Reading "Lady Lazarus" carefully will help you see some of those references and likely provide some "aha" moments when you are thinking about possible topics for papers.

One thing to help you keep an eye out for the statements Plath is making is to find out more about her as a writer. Plath desire to write about "'taboo' subject matter and 'emotional and psychological depth' were the artistic aims she designated for all of her writing" (Middlebrook 200). Her goals were not merely to document her own life and experiences for all to see—she was trying to challenge accepted strategies and expectations in both the literary world and the culture around her. That desire to startle readers is evident in this poem, where she talks bluntly about suicide as well as incorporating images from the Holocaust. Many readers and critics have been angered by the Holocaust imagery in Plath's poems, notably "Lady Lazarus" and "Daddy," feeling she has no right to claim affiliation with the victims of the genocide, as it seems she does in lines 5 through 9 in the poem.

Once again, though, reading through a different lens can help you see what Plath might have been trying to do with these images. Ann Keniston argues that "the Holocaust in 'Lady Lazarus' does not appear as a conflict or even as a historical event. . . . What persists in 'Lady Lazarus' is the body of the victim, nearly distinct from that of the enemy or the doctor she only a few times addresses" (Keniston 147). In other words, some readers believe Plath is not claiming to be a victim on par with victims of the Holocaust, which is what many of those readers who get angry are claiming she is doing. Instead, she is using the Holocaust, a well-recognized instance of heinous and senseless human cruelty, to bring what she sees as other atrocities to light.

The first lines of the poem demonstrate not only what upsets critics about this poem, but also what can be ferreted out by a close reading of an excerpt of the work:

> I have done it again.
> One year in every ten
> I manage it—
>
> A sort of walking miracle, my skin
> Bright as a Nazi lampshade,
> My right foot

A paperweight,
My face a featureless, fine
Jew linen.

Peel off the napkin
O my enemy.
Do I terrify?—

As you can see, references to Nazis and Jews stand out immediately. However, rather than just stopping there and assuming Plath is comparing herself to one of the victims of the Holocaust, considering the delivery of those images can help you to come up with a more complex understanding of this passage, which is helpful in an essay.

One way to gain that more complex understanding is to think about why Plath brings up this horrible chapter in world history. Ann Keniston suggests, "Plath reinforces her speakers' removal from the Holocaust" as a way to make readers realize how removed they also are from it; the speaker here "represent[s] the Holocaust as corrupted, and the corruption of the figures themselves reveals the failure of conventional poetic mechanisms of representation in relation to the Holocaust" (143). In other words, by bringing these images into her poem, Plath is actually pointing out how ill-equipped people are to talk about horrible events like these. When she urges readers to "Peel off the napkin" (14), she realizes they will be terrified by what they see. By introducing subject matter and images like this into her poetry, Plath is trying to jolt readers into understanding how distanced they are from these events and therefore how difficult it is to talk about them with any sort of truth or even empathy.

The introduction of political statements, especially about World War II and the cold war, are nothing new for Plath. She had great fears about what might become of the world if the cold war gave way to another world war, and her journals feature many entries where she voices her concern and anger over decisions and policies made by both her native United States and her adopted England. As you think about this poem and how to write about it, keep these issues in mind. When Plath talks about death or suicide, she is not always only talking about her own; consider how the personal things she brings up can be contextualized by what was going on in the world around her.

TOPICS AND STRATEGIES

The following ideas are meant to give you a place to start. When you read the questions after each suggestion for a topic, think about why you answer the way you do. Do not stop at just answering the question; find specific examples in the text of "Lady Lazarus" that influenced your answers. Supplying textual evidence for a point or assertion you make helps to support that point and also helps to clarify it for your readers.

It is important not to let all the hype about Sylvia Plath influence your reading of her work in a way that limits your ability to think of original and interesting essay topics. That she committed suicide is a fact, and that her work sometimes even documents her attempts at suicide and her personal anguish at the death of her father and the breakup of her marriage is also a fact. But, it is an equally important fact that Plath was a poet, which means that she was not simply journaling her life in her work; she was creating something that would communicate a message to readers.

Themes

As you look for themes to use for an essay project, think about how you reacted to the poem and what you think made you react that way. For instance, were you confused? If so, what do you need to know in order to clear things up for you? Poetry can seem daunting to write about for some students because the messages in it do not seem as clear cut as they are in other works of fiction. Rereading a poem is key to overcoming this. If you read carefully through a poem several times, you can often find some messages tucked into the text that you missed in the first couple of times you read it.

There are some themes in "Lady Lazarus" that Plath addresses in other works, too. Although it is important to refrain from assuming that everything Plath writes about has to do with death, especially hers, death is something that deserves to be looked at in this poem. But be careful not to get so caught up in looking for major issues that you miss references to emotions and other parts of human nature. Think about what Plath is talking about in this poem that is sort of universal, part of the human experience. Looking at the poem from that angle might help you

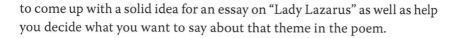

to come up with a solid idea for an essay on "Lady Lazarus" as well as help you decide what you want to say about that theme in the poem.

Sample Topics:

1. **Women and power:** What is being said about women's power in this poem? Is this a poem of a woman becoming empowered?

Many readers see this poem as an attack against all men; but Tracy Brain argues that's too simple a reading; "For many critics and biographers, the final lines of 'Lady Lazarus' . . . represent Sylvia Plath's own stance on men . . . [she] dislikes men, is positively dangerous to them" (119). How would you argue that the last lines of the poem are actually about the speaker taking control of her life? Where in the poem do you see the speaker pointing to times when someone, especially Herr Doktor, had control over her? Is death the only power the speaker has? What does the speaker mean when she says "I am your opus, / I am your valuable, / The pure gold baby" (67–69)? Is this an inference that she is a possession? What would you say the speaker is saying about women and men in this poem? In the end, is she a hateful maneater? Has she saved herself?

2. **Fire and ashes:** What exactly is getting burned away? What is significant about what is left in the ashes after the fire?

One obvious image in this poem is that of the phoenix that rises from the ashes, especially prominent in the last several lines. Why do you think the items that are left in the ashes are "A cake of soap, / A wedding ring, / A gold filling" (76–78)? How are those especially meaningful in light of her words aimed at Herr Doktor? Another reference to fire and ash comes in the beginning of the poem when Plath mentions Nazis and Jews. What connotations do readers have about fire when they see those specific terms? Are there different kinds of fire in this poem? Is fire something to fear, or is it a purifying force?

3. **Death:** Is death something to strive for or something to overcome in this poem?

Al Alvarez says of Plath, "Death was a debt to be met once every decade: in order to stay alive . . . she had to pay . . . with her life . . . it was a passionate act, instinct as much with love as with hatred and despair . . . [it]becomes an invocation of some deadly ritual" (197). Where do you see the description of that ritual in the poem? Do you see this notion of death as a debt to be paid in this poem? What is the significance of paying the debt every decade? How does the description of the second death in "Lady Lazarus" in lines 37 through 42 mirror Plath's own attempt during her second decade of life? Is there a certain honor or power in controlling the circumstances of one's own death? Or is death seen as a better option than what society has in store for the speaker?

4. **Defiance:** What cultural expectations is the speaker in this poem defying?

Wagner-Martin argues that this poem shows "the persona moving from her conventional state of social acceptance to the flourish of triumph, no matter how unconventional her behavior has become" (111). What unconventional behavior has the speaker in this poem exhibited? Wagner-Martin goes on to say the speaker is "a woman who readily defies death to taunt the society that would contain, and constrain her" (111). How does her excellence at the art of dying taunt society? Does her survival further insult society, or is it a sign of her inability to completely rid herself of society's constraints? Annas believes this poem is "about the relation between the poet and a society which consistently defines her in a way she feels to be false" (158). What in the poem indicates how society is defining her? How is it false?

Characters

When faced with the question, "Who are the characters in this poem?" students sometimes become frustrated; unlike novels and short stories where characters are easy to identify, finding specific voices and characters in poetry can be tough. In "Lady Lazarus," there are even more options to answer that question than are offered below. The following suggestions are just that—suggestions. You might find there are other characters in this poem that you wish to focus on; if you do, you might use the questions from this section to help you develop your thoughts for an essay about that character or those characters.

Sample Topics:

1. **The speaker:** How would you argue that the speaker of this poem is not actually Sylvia Plath?

   Who, then, is the "I" in the poem? Tracy Brain expresses disappointment at readers, especially novice readers, who cannot separate the poet from her work, lamenting that "Frequently in essays, students will go so far as to refer to the narrators of poems as 'Plath'" (11). Why is this a problem? What happens to the analysis of a poem when a reader automatically assumes the poet is the speaker of the work? One of the reasons Brain believes readers make such an assumption is the overwhelming tendency of even critics and scholars to assume Plath is the "I" in all of her work. How does that assumption make Plath's work seem more or less the result of careful crafting? Could you argue that making that assumption actually makes it easier for readers as they try to work through Plath's poetry and prose?

2. **Lady Lazarus:** Who exactly is the Lady Lazarus of the poem's title?

   Is Lady Lazarus an alter ego for the speaker in the poem? Kroll sees this poem as one of several that "directly consider the ego or selfhood as the problem" for someone trying to abandon the self to achieve transcendence (177). What part of her self is Lady Lazarus trying to shed? Will the speaker be shed in this process? Or is the speaker trying to shed Lady Lazarus? If Lady Lazarus and the speaker are not one and the same, why the use of first person in the poem? Could Lady Lazarus be a sacrificial figure—one the speaker can offer up to the masses as a way to satisfy them without sacrificing herself? Who do you believe has the stronger voice, the speaker or Lady Lazarus? Or do they speak in concert?

3. **The listener/reader:** Who do you think Plath wanted to hear this poem? Who was she trying to "get to" in "Lady Lazarus"?

Many critics and readers feel Plath was writing this poem as a sort of indictment of her husband and his infidelity. But there is also an argument to be made that she is writing this to the culture at large. Based on your reading of the poem, who do you think Plath is addressing in this poem? What images or references in the poem make you answer this way? Ann Keniston believes Plath knew her poem would elicit strong response from readers, claiming she "anticipated her readers' . . . response to her poems, and . . . as these readers have responded both ravenously and contemptuously to her self-revelations, they have fulfilled a role Plath already scripted for them" (153). How would you support this statement, based on your reading of the poem?

History and Context

The 1950s were important years in the development of the treatment for mental illness. In 1953, H.M. (his name was withheld to preserve his privacy) was admitted to the hospital with epilepsy; eventually, in an effort to treat the seizures, surgeons cauterized his brain. The seizures stopped, his IQ remained unchanged, but he developed a form of amnesia that left him unable to remember anything from that point in his life forward (Barrett). His case was famous because it brought public attention to the practice of brain surgery and altering the brain to alter behavior.

In 1953 Plath received electroconvulsive therapy (ECT), which entails running electrical currents through the brain. ECT would have interrupted brain development in someone her age, whose brain was still developing. ECT is still performed, but it is as a last resort; medication and therapy are used first. Plath's lifetime saw a sea change in how mental illness was considered and treated; operating on the brain gave way to medication and improved treatment (Barrett).

Because of the time period, and because of Plath's own treatments for depression, it is likely she would have been at least familiar with the case of H.M. The field of neuroscience was in its infancy in the 1950s, and at least partially due to H.M., there was a movement away from tinkering with the brain like that (Barrett). The brain would have been a real mystery during Plath's lifetime, unlike today when people talk confidently about learning styles, left and right brain activities, and other things about the brain. As you think about the historical context for Plath's work, consider not only her personal history but medical and cultural history, as well, to help you come up with ideas for an essay.

Sample Topics:

1. **Treatment for mental illness:** How would Sylvia Plath be treated for depression if she were alive now? Do you think that would have an effect on her work?

   During the Civil War era in the United States, the census included questions about whether there was anyone who was "insane or an idiot" living in the home, leaving it up to family members to "diagnose" such a condition (Barrett). How does that idea of one's family deciding whether they are sane or not apply to Plath? Where does that come through in "Lady Lazarus"? Plath's depression is so well established that psychologist Dr. James Kaufman discovered a connection between depression and creativity he calls the Sylvia Plath Effect. How do you think Plath's suicide and bold writing about it has influenced popular opinion about the connection between madness and creativity? How has Plath's suicide especially influenced ideas about the tortured female artist?

2. **Suicide:** What do you think Plath is saying about her own attempts at suicide in this poem?

   When Plath talked about her suicide attempts, more often than not it made her an outsider, yet she seemed to almost relish the experience: "I feel like Lazarus; that story has such a fascination. Being dead, I rose up again, and even resort to the mere sensation value of being suicidal, of getting so close, of coming out of the grave with the scars and the marring mark on my cheek which (is it my imagination?) grows more prominent." (qtd. in Stevenson 71) How does this quote from Plath affect your understanding of "Lady Lazarus"? Does Plath here seem to wear her suicide attempts as a badge of honor? How is Lady Lazarus an outsider for speaking about her attempts at dying? How is she empowered by that control over life and death?

3. **Woman as professional writer:** What images support a reading of this poem as a statement about the difficulties faced by Plath as a woman poet in a literary world dominated by men?

   How do you see Plath flexing her artistic muscles in this poem? Linda Wagner-Martin argues that the speaker in the poem is proud; "She is good at her profession (which is attempting suicide), and in a society that allows women so few distinctions, hers is significant" (221). How does a profession of killing herself connect to a profession as a writer? What parts of Lady Lazarus are her own, and which have been put on her? Bundtzen sees Lady Lazarus as a sort of Frankenstein's monster—as the female artist put together by Herr Doktor and Herr God (a patriarchal literary system) who depend on her willingness to go along with their plan (34). How does Plath show her refusal to go along with that plan? Is she successful in this refusal?

Form and Genre

Tracy Brain warns against reading this and other of Plath's works as mere autobiography:

The premise is that to explain the life, readers can look at the work. Reciprocally, to explain the work, "they can turn to the life" and thus, all of Plath, her life and her work, are boiled down too easily to a quick story that reads 'Plath falls in love with Ted Hughes, they have two children, their marriage breaks down, and she dies.' (20)

Part of the temptation to read Plath's work this way might also stem from the fact that her poetry most often fits in the genre of confessional poetry, a style of poetry where the poet incorporates personal experience in her or his work. Importantly, though, confessional poetry is not just about talking about one's self—it is also about using those experiences as a way to say something more, to talk about something larger than oneself. As you think about possible topics for an essay or other project about "Lady Lazarus," consider how you would recognize confessional poetry. Do you need to know about the poet's life in order to recognize a confessional poem? If "Lady Lazarus" is a confessional poem, as most critics believe, where does the personal experience make way for the statement about those larger issues?

Sample Topics:

1. **Voice:** Is there just one voice in this poem? Whose voice dominates this poem?

   How does this poem exemplify Plath's poetic voice? Where do you see the confessional part of the poetry coming through? Plath's mother, Aurelia, published a book of the letters her daughter wrote her, partially to illustrate that Sylvia was not always the tormented soul people see in her poetry. She writes in the book, "The haunting memories of emotional terror voiced in some of the poems were in direct contrast to the strong, affirmative voice she gave forth in her letters and conversations with her family" (Plath, Aurelia 359). How might you explain that radical difference in the voice of the poet and the voice of the daughter? Which would you believe is the most authentic of the two voices? What does that say about how purposefully Plath created a voice for her poetry that was not necessarily always her own?

2. **The villanelle:** How would you argue that this poem qualifies as a villanelle? How would you argue that it does not?

   A villanelle is a specific style of poem that is typically nineteen lines long, with specific rhyme patterns. Although this poem does not follow the pattern completely, Plath's poetry is considered by many to be a contemporary form of the villanelle ("Poetic Form"). How has Plath updated the villanelle for a twentieth-century audience? What do you think might have intrigued Plath about the villanelle style? What about the subject matter fits the form? In her journal, Plath writes "I rail and rage against the taking of my father, whom I have never known; even his mind, his heart, his face. . . . My villanelle was to my father; and the best one" (Kukil 230). How does Plath's use of the form in "Daddy" compare with her use of it in "Lady Lazarus"?

3. **Reading Aloud:** What patterns and emphases emerge when you read the poem out loud? How does reading the poem out loud change or influence your understanding of the poem?

Pamela Annas sees this poem as having "the vocal quality of a manifesto" (136). How is the power of the message of this poem emphasized by reading it out loud? How would you describe the difference between reading "Lady Lazarus" silently and reading it out loud? About the poems in the *Ariel* collection, Plath said in a BBC interview, "they are written for the ear, not the eye: they are poems written out loud" (Plath, *Ariel* 193). How would you characterize the difference between a poem that's written for the eye and one written for the ear? Do you see any similarity between what the poem looks like on the page and how it sounds?

Philosophy and Ideas

Diane Middlebrook, author of a book about Plath and Ted Hughes, notes that Plath wanted to "write works that were 'relevant to the larger things, the bigger things such as Hiroshima and Dachau'" (200). Many readers become distracted by the way her writing relates to her personal experiences and overlook the "bigger things" that Plath is addressing in her poetry. As you consider the ideas mentioned in the following section, reread the poem and try to set aside the things that feel autobiographical and see if you can dig around a little deeper to discover what other contexts Plath might have been working within. Remember that confessional poetry, the genre most closely associated with Plath, is not just about telling your story; it also emphasizes using that story to make a larger statement about something. Look for those issues and statements Plath is making by sharing her experiences in this poem.

Sample Topics:

1. **Rebirth and/or resurrection:** In this poem, how does the speaker characterize her survivals after her attempts at dying?

   The Lazarus reference conjures up images of resurrection. What is the difference between resurrection and rebirth? Which do you think Lady Lazarus thinks she has undergone? Wagner-Martin draws attention to the fact that the time when Plath wrote this poem "is the ending of Plath's long and debilitating saga of pain . . . she had reached a kind of reconciliation with herself, though she was worn and anguished from the struggle" (221). How does the act of reconciling with oneself relate to rebirth? Kroll points to the striptease in this poem; the bandages that are removed can also be seen as a symbol of rebirth; mummies were preserved that way for an expected rebirth, as well (161). Do you think Lady Lazarus will die again and be reborn again? What examples from the text would you use to support your answer to that question?

2. **Gender:** Is this poem a feminist poem? What in the text of the poem leads you to your answer to that question?

   What expectations for women do you see Plath addressing in this poem? What is Lady Lazarus saying about those roles? Do you think Lady Lazarus and Plath are of the same opinion about how women are treated? Tracy Brain warns against instantly assuming all of Plath's writing carries a strident feminist message:

   > Plath has often been accused of using her writing to express anger at men, and in particular her resentment of her father

and husband. . . . Such . . . misreading overlooks Plath's concern that men as well as women are put under terrible pressures to comply with the rules and constraints imposed upon
them by their gender. (3)

How would you respond to Brain about her argument? In
"Lady Lazarus" where do you see references to the roles both
men and women are expected to fulfill? What is Plath saying
about those roles? Would you identify one of the genders, male
or female, as being in control in this poem? What has Lady
Lazarus done, or not done, to help establish that control by
one of the genders?

3. **"Bigger things":** What political and cultural statements do you
think Plath is making in this poem?

How does Plath use the persona of Lady Lazarus and her experiences to point out flaws in society and societal expectations?
Pamela Annas argues Plath is pointing out societal apathy in
this poem, especially through the speaker, who

> equates herself with the Jewish victims of Nazi Germany and
> the crowd, that is, us, with those who watched, horrified but
> implicated in the act because for a long time we did nothing
> to stop it, since, we thought, it had nothing to do with us. The
> deader, more dehumanized, more isolated people become, the
> more horror it takes to elicit any kind of response (138).

How could Plath's background as an American who moved
to England play into this idea of apathy? Who is she saying
should have done something sooner? What other issues is
she suggesting the crowd is turning a blind eye to? Even the
idea of resurrection carries an implication of commercial-
ity in this poem; "Once the . . . spectacle is over, the clothes
strewn in Lady Lazarus's striptease, like the shroud left in the
tomb by Christ's risen body, will be sold as religious relics with
special healing and restorative powers" (Bundtzen 29). How

does incorporating religion and religious imagery into the poem help Plath make her point about the "peanut-crunching crowd" that needs to be shocked into action and even then does not always lend a hand?

4. **Survival:** How does the speaker feel about surviving her attempts to die?

How do her suicide attempts help to define the speaker? How do they help to determine her future? Plath told her friend, poet and critic Al Alvarez, about her suicide attempts, including one in which she had run her car off the road. After Plath's death, he wrote of the incident, saying

> It had been no accident; she had gone off the road deliberately, seriously, wanting to die. But she hadn't, and all that was now in the past. For this reason, I am convinced that at this time she was not contemplating suicide. On the contrary, she was able to write about the act so freely because it was already behind her. (196)

Based on reading this poem, would you support Alvarez's assertion about his friend or not? Is Plath using Lady Lazarus as a voice to express her triumph at surviving her attempts at ending her life? After reading the poem, do you feel that the speaker is going to live triumphantly or finally succeed in ending her life?

Language, Images, and Symbolism

There are some fairly obvious images and symbols to choose for a paper about this poem, and some of them are discussed in this section. As you choose a topic to write an essay about, though, try not to think only about the things that jump out at most readers; reread the poem and consider those images or language choices you find particularly compelling. Sometimes coming up with something not as obvious can prove to be the most rewarding path to take for a writing project. If you do decide to write about one of the notable images or symbols Plath uses in this poem, remember to think about digging deeper. Rather than just introducing readers to the fact that Plath includes this or that image in the poem, remember that you should also think about the *why* behind those choices made by the poet.

Sample Topics:

1. **Body parts:** What is symbolized by the various parts of the body mentioned in "Lady Lazarus"?

   In the first few lines, the poet says she is "A sort of walking miracle" (4) and then describes a sort of Frankenstein's monster assortment of body parts. A few lines later there is mention of "The nose, the eye pits, the full set of teeth" (13) and then "the flesh / The grave cave ate" (16–17). Do you think the emphasis is on taking apart a body or putting one together? In what condition is the body of Lady Lazarus? Who is responsible for that condition? Later in the poem there are references to other parts of the body, including skin, bones, heart, blood, and hair. Since Plath is well known for her careful choices of words and images, it can be assumed these specific parts were chosen for a reason. What do you see as a common thread between all of them? How might the parts of the body mentioned in the poem contribute to a larger statement Plath is making?

2. **Christianity:** How are Lady Lazarus's recoveries after her suicide attempts likened to resurrection?

   There is a clear reference in this poem to Christian ideas about resurrection in the use of the name *Lazarus*. Lynda Bundtzen reads the poem this way:

   > Christian symbolism is yoked with three other actions: the sideshow striptease; the suffering inflicted by the Nazis on the Jews; and the personal acts of self-destruction compulsively repeated each decade. Plath stresses the public nature of the

spectacle, so that her suicide attempts are no more private or personal than the Oberammergau Passion Play and its ritualized repetition of Christ's crucifixion and resurrection every ten years. Lady Lazarus's suffering is also a religious calling, a vocation. Her comeback is a 'miracle' like Christ's resurrection of Lazarus (29).

How does reading this excerpt from Bundtzen change your understanding of this poem? What do you think Plath is saying about Christianity in this poem? She was raised as a Unitarian Universalist and attended church when she was living in Devon, so she was no stranger to religion and spirituality. What might she be saying about her own beliefs? What might she be trying to get readers to consider about their own beliefs?

3. **War and the Holocaust:** What message is Plath trying to send by incorporating Holocaust imagery into this poem?

Why use the specific images she does in this poem to get this message across? Ann Keniston believes that "Plath looks at the Holocaust from the estranged position of the nonsurvivor; her speakers are impelled back to a Holocaust they insist cannot be represented" (154). What might Plath be hoping readers will think about when they read these references to Nazis and Jews? What injustice could she have been trying to point out to readers by bringing in these references? What group or groups could she have been saying are being wrongfully treated by another? How might she have seen what she was going through in her own life as a sort of holocaust? How might she have seen her mother Aurelia as perpetrating a kind of holocaust on her childhood?

4. **Onlookers:** What role do the onlookers and spectators play in this poem? How might this relate to Plath's feelings about people pitying her because of her divorce and worrying about her because of her previous suicide attempts?

Do you think Plath was referencing how she was being watched by others, with pity and discomfort, like a freak in a circus sideshow, because of her split from Ted Hughes? How does the reference to the "peanut-crunching crowd" (26) characterize those onlookers? Lynda Bundtzen argues that "[t]here is a perpetual antagonism between Lady Lazarus and her spectators, as though she wants and needs their sympathy, but will laugh in their faces if they dare to pity her. And so she both appeals to them and insults them with her casual attitude toward atrocity" (31). How do you see that attitude as congruent with Plath's own feelings about those around her? What other contexts could Plath be using for this tension between spectacle and spectators? What is she saying about how a person is seen and talked about after he or she is dead?

Compare and Contrast

As always, there are many choices to be made when deciding on works to use for a compare and contrast essay. Those listed below incorporate what seems like a fairly obvious choice, comparing this poem to other works by Plath, but there is also an idea for incorporating something from film into a compare and contrast paper. Considering cultural, and even popular culture, artifacts from the time period in which a piece of literature was written can be useful to you as you plan an essay in which you compare and contrast. Think about whether you want to address what readers at the time would have been familiar with or hearing about on the news or whether you want to address things that contemporary readers, like you, would know. This can help you to more clearly focus on what sorts of pieces you want to use in a compare and contrast essay.

Sample Topics:

1. **"Lady Lazarus" and "Nick and the Candlestick":** How do you see these poems as illustrating her feelings about motherhood versus her feelings about being a wife?

   These poems are written during the same time period, yet their tones are entirely different. What do you think that means about what was going on in Plath's life at the time?

Both poems seem pointed at a male audience; "Lady Lazarus" ends with a kind of warning to men, maybe even her estranged husband, ("And I eat men like air"), and "Nick and the Candlestick" ends with a worshipful note ("You are the baby in the barn"). What do you think this says about how Plath hoped her son would turn out? How does the hopeful message in "Nick and the Candlestick" complicate assertions that the *Ariel* collection is a clear indication of her suicidal thoughts? Why do you think that "Lady Lazarus" is the more talked about poem of the two? Do you think "Lady Lazarus" feeds into readers' expectations about Plath's mental state more than "Nick and the Candlestick"? How so, or how not?

2. **Lady Lazarus to the biblical Lazarus:** There is an obvious biblical connection here, just because of the use of the name *Lazarus*. What specifically, though, do you think Plath was trying to get across by making her character in this poem *Lady* Lazarus?

Plath upsets the biblical story of Lazarus by changing the figure to a woman in this poem. What specific details from the story of Lazarus are included in this poem? How are they used to tell the story of Lady Lazarus? Where does Plath veer away from the specifics of the Bible story? Based on your reading of the poem, how familiar was Plath with the story? Do you think she used it as an inspiration or as something to work against? Was she trying to upset readers by using the name *Lazarus?* Thinking back to those assertions that Plath was trying to address bigger issues in her work, what issue or issues do you think Plath might have been trying to tackle here?

3. **Electricity and peanuts in "Lady Lazarus" and *The Bell Jar*:** What is signified by the connection between electricity and peanuts in these two works?

In the opening lines of *The Bell Jar*, Esther Greenwood talks about the electrocution of the Rosenbergs. She also mentions "the fusty, peanut-smelling mouth of every subway" (1). In this poem, Plath references "a million filaments" (25) and "The peanut-crunching crowd" (26). Why pair these two things? How do they work the same or differently in each of these works? Is electricity something to fear or something that demonstrates power? Does it open the door to rebirth, or does it kill? How might the idea of the peanut crunchers in the poem be applied to the smell of peanuts in the subway? Is Plath implying something about spectacle in these two? Is Lady Lazarus undergoing a sort of electrocution, as did the Rosenbergs and even Esther (through her electroconvulsive therapy) in the novel?

4. **"Lady Lazarus" and *Vertigo*:** How is the notion of rebirth treated in each of these works? How are the women in each of the works created by the men around them?

In *Vertigo*, the female lead is two women; she is her self and also the "reincarnation" of a dead woman, hired by a man who killed his wife to masquerade as his wife and pretend to be killed by suicide. Key to her masquerade is an apparent *attempt* to kill herself, from which she recovers. How does this theme compare to the theme in "Lady Lazarus"? In the film, the woman hired by the husband undergoes a transformation at the hands of another man, who had fallen in love with her during her masquerade. How does Lady Lazarus undergo the same sort of transformation? How does the idea of resurrection apply in each of these works? How do both of them hinge on the idea of the woman being mentally unstable enough to kill herself? Why is that significant in these two works?

Bibliography and Online Resources for "Lady Lazarus"

Alvarez, A. "Sylvia Plath: A Memoir." *Ariel Ascending: Writings About Sylvia Plath*. Ed. Paul Alexander. New York: Harper and Row, 1985.

Barrett, Terence, Ph.D. Personal interview. 17 Dec. 2010.

Brain, Tracy. *The Other Sylvia Plath*. Harlow, England: Pearson, 2001. Print.

Bundtzen, Lynda. *Plath's Incarnations: Woman and the Creative Process*. Ann Arbor, MI: U of Michigan P, 1983. Print.

Hughes, Frieda. Foreword. ix–xvii. Plath, Sylvia. *Ariel*. Restored ed. London: Faber and Faber, 2004. Print.

Keniston, Ann. "The Holocaust Again: Sylvia Plath, Belatedness, and the Limits of Lyric Figure." *The Unraveling Archive: Essays on Sylvia Plath*. Anita Helle, ed. Ann Arbor, MI: U of MI P, 2007. 139–57. Print.

Kroll, Judith. *Chapters in a Mythology: The Poetry of Sylvia Plath*. New York: Harper and Row, 1976. Print.

Middlebrook, Diane. *Her Husband: Ted Hughes and Sylvia Plath. A Marriage*. New York: Penguin, 2003. Print.

Plath, Sylvia. *The Bell Jar*. New York: Harper Collins, 1971. Print.

———. "Lady Lazarus." *Ariel: The Restored Edition*. London: Faber and Faber, 2004. Print.

"Poetic Form: Villanelle." *Poets.org*. The Academy of American Poets. n.d. Web. 15 Aug. 2010.

Stevenson, Anne. *Bitter Fame: A Life of Sylvia Plath*. Boston: Houghton Mifflin, 1989. Print.

Wagner-Martin, Linda. *Sylvia Plath: A Biography*. New York: Simon and Schuster, 1987. Print.

THREE WOMEN

READING TO WRITE

Sylvia Plath's *Three Women* aired on BBC radio on August 19, 1962; many critics and biographers see the seeds of the famous *Ariel* collection in this work. Plath herself added the subtitle "A Poem for Three Voices," but the work is most often referred to as a play. This work and *The Bell Jar* were among the last works Plath wrote before her death in 1963, along with the poems that would famously be called the *Ariel* collection. This play, although written at about the same time as those famous poems, was included in a collection called *Winter Trees* that was edited and arranged by her husband, Ted Hughes, and published after Plath's death.

When Plath originally wrote *Three Women*, the women in the play each had a name; as her work on the project continued, she took out names and in the final version they are Voice One, Voice Two, and Voice Three, also known as the Wife, the Secretary, and the Girl (Wagner-Martin, *Biography* 199). As Wagner-Martin also notes:

> What Plath achieves in choosing three different kinds of pregnancies—one miscarriage, one full-term delivery in which the unmarried mother would give the baby up for adoption, and one delivery in which the mother would take the child and raise it—is the canvas for a spectrum of physical experiences and attitudes. (*Literary Life* 100).

Like much of Plath's other work, this play has a confessional air about it. Plath's own history included a miscarriage and the birth of two children, so she was likely drawing from her own life when she wrote this play, even though neither of Plath's two babies was born in a hospital. As you read the play to look for essay topics, it is important to remember the confessional nature of Plath's work, but also to realize that this play is not necessarily autobiographical, even if it is tempting to read it as such.

The first voice, that of the wife, is the one that is clearly most celebratory about motherhood. But even in that voice there are occasional hints of the problems that motherhood presents for women, even those who are happy to have children. She wonders:

> How long can I be a wall, keeping the wind off?
> How long can I be
> Gentling the sun with the shade of my hand,
> Intercepting the blue bolts of a cold moon?
> The voices of loneliness, the voices of sorrow
> Lap at my back ineluctably.
> How shall it soften them, this little lullaby?
>
> How can I be a wall around my green property?
> How long can my hands
> Be a bandage to his hurt, and my words
> Bright birds in the sky, consoling, consoling?
> It is a terrible thing
> To be so open: it is as if my heart
> Put on a face and walked into the world. (Plath 185)

As Lynda Bundtzen notes, for this woman, "the delivery itself is a cruel miracle that arouses questions" about the possible trouble that will come with mothering a child (212). Even as she celebrates the birth of her child, she is already frightened at the thought of what could happen to him when she can no longer protect him and he is out in the world.

Within this concern the wife has for her son's future can be seen some of Plath's own concerns about the environment and the political climate into which she brought her own children. Throughout her journals are mentions of her fears stemming from the cold war of the 1950s; she writes of the bombing of Nagasaki, "God save us from doing that again" and fears that "[w]ar will come some day now, with all the hothead leaders and articles" (Kukil 46). Tracy Brain argues that, although confessional, Plath's work also tackles myriad social issues, especially environmental ones, and that "Much of Plath's writing hinges on exchanges within a global ecosystem that includes the climate, the soil, the air, animal life, and the individual human body" (84). This attention to the natural is obvious in this section of the poem, as well, when Plath uses the images of the natural as metaphors for the troubles and strife that she knows will ultimately await her newborn son.

Along with those dangers are the emotional dangers the wife knows her son will face, "The voices of loneliness, the voices of sorrow" (Plath 185) that the mother has apparently heard herself. The mother, ecstatic to have given birth to this lovely boy, even as she first holds him ponders the ills that the world has in store for him. This sense of melancholy mingled with her joy creates a real sense of the types of problems Plath saw in the world into which she brought her own children and especially her son, Nicholas, who was born shortly before this play was written. It also demonstrates a sense of social responsibility on Plath's part; she wrote to her mother about her joy in taking her daughter, Frieda, to a ban-the-bomb march when she was a baby, happy that her daughter's first little "adventure" was a protest against "the insanity of world-domination" (Plath, *Letters Home* 378).

As you decide on topics for essays, consider the bigger picture into which Plath was placing this play. Read for clues about the social issues and problems that she saw as especially affecting the institution of motherhood. Keep in mind Brain's argument that Plath possessed a "complex view of men's and women's shared places in this system" and that this view "contradicts the still prevalent view of Plath as self-obsessed" (84). Consider, instead, what Plath might have been trying to accomplish in terms of social change through her writing.

TOPICS AND STRATEGIES

This work offers some different avenues for exploring topics because it is a play, and most students are likely much more familiar with her novel, *The Bell Jar*, and her poetry than they are this play. As you decide on a topic for an essay about this work, you might want to keep in mind how you see this as a hybrid; its subtitle in Plath's *Collected Poems* is "A Poem for Three Voices" (176). Thus, even though it was produced and performed as a radio play, you can also use some of the techniques and strategies you use to think about poetry to determine an approach to writing about *Three Women*. As always, it is important to look below the surface when you are deciding on a topic for an essay; relying on one reading is not sufficient. And, given Plath's insistence that her work was meant to be read out loud, it is also important that you do that with this work in order to more fully understand some of the intricacies of the work and the effects Plath hoped it would have on readers and listeners.

Themes

Motherhood is perhaps the strongest theme in this play, but as you consider an essay topic, you should also think about the complexities of motherhood being addressed in this play. Many readers and critics see *Three Women* as a testament to motherhood, especially since the wife character is the one who is the most fulfilled. Even the student, who seems "happy to return to her freedom, ends with the question, 'What is it I miss?'" (Bundtzen 214). Along with the secretary's despair at not being able to give birth, the student's response serves to heighten the sense that Plath is portraying motherhood as a noble and happy event in a woman's life. It is important to read carefully for the messages Plath is sending about how motherhood is influenced by the world in which the mother lives and works, which can open up a number of other avenues to explore for an essay topic.

Sample Topics:

1. **Motherhood:** What does motherhood give to the mother? What does it take away? How are those answers demonstrated in the responses of the three voices?

   How do the personal lives of the three women in the play influence how they view motherhood? Is motherhood seen as a necessary part of being a woman? Bundtzen argues, "The balance of the poem . . . is in favor of the smug, irrefutable wisdom of the mother" (214); do you see the main statement of the poem being about the joy of motherhood? Plath wrote to her mother about Nick, "I really *enjoy* him—none of the harassment and worry of Frieda's colic and my inexperience. I love playing with him, and I also am rested enough to find energy to play with Frieda in the second half of the day" (*Letters Home* 447–48). How do you think Plath's own experiences with motherhood are illustrated in this play?

2. **Creativity:** How are the women in this play being alienated from their creations? How is that separation related to the culture in which they live?

   Pamela Annas argues this play "is about what stands in the way of creativity . . . in a bureaucratized society that confuses the word with the thing" and "a capitalistic society that alienates the producer from what is produced, including babies" (73–74). How is creativity portrayed in this play? How does the lack of communication among the three women help to demonstrate how creativity is affected by cultural expectations? How are the women's views of themselves affected by what they create or what they fail to create?

3. **Mechanization:** What role do machines play in *Three Women*? How does mechanization affect the women in this play?

   The secretary "merges with the machine, ordering parts, while her body gives itself over to a natural process—death" (Bundtzen 217). What is the correlation between a mechanized world and the failure of the natural process of childbirth? Why is that mechanized world equated with men rather than women? Bundtzen argues, "The man's misunderstanding of what is happening [to the secretary] is the result of his 'de-natured' environment 'fit only for machines to live in'" (217). How does the man misunderstand the secretary's pregnancy? How is that a product of his overly mechanized world?

4. **Patriarchal control of motherhood:** What role do men play in the feelings the three women in this play have about motherhood?

One critic sees Plath making pointed statements about the patriarchal system in this poem, noting a sense that "The woman's womb is an empty space to be filled by the man" (Bundtzen 215). Even though there are no men who are characters in this play, how is that patriarchal system present in this work? What examples do the characters provide that demonstrate their understanding of men's roles in motherhood? What is the significance of the most "successful" of the three mothers giving birth to a baby boy? Where do you see patriarchal control playing a role in the secretary's inability to become a mother? How might her husband's patience with her also illustrate this kind of control? "The antagonism between mind and body is between man and woman, God and nature. The man thinks and acts, the woman bears the consequences. His are the ends, but hers are the means" (Bundtzen 215).

Characters

The characters in this play present an interesting cross-section of the female experience of birth. Arguably, the first voice, the wife, is the heroine of the story. Bundtzen writes, "She is so much the stereotypical earth mother that she fights off intuitions of future sorrow and blindly turns away from the real world" (212) and notes that "The secretary and student provide ironic counterpoint to the earth mother's confidence and complacency" (Bundtzen 212). Undoubtedly there are confessional notes in this play; Plath's own experiences with birth and miscarriage do enter into this play in obvious ways. Wagner-Martin writes, "As focused as the text manages to be on the three child-bearing women and their poetry, their responses to the life events that are handed to them, fated for them, elements of Plath's own life at the time manage to creep in" (*Literary Life* 102).

As you consider a topic for an essay about a character from this poem, think carefully about the ways in which the three women featured in this play are different and also the ways in which they are alike. You might also want to think about how Plath is using the setting of the maternity ward as a tactic for emphasizing those differences and similarities.

Sample Topics:

1. **First Voice:** How would you characterize the distinctive voice of the First Voice? How does she fit the ideal earth mother, happy with all that motherhood entails?

   How is it significant that the married woman who bears a child is the first voice readers see or listeners hear? Do you think that Plath, as a wife and mother, treats the voice of the wife differently than that of the other two? Does it seem more like her own voice to you? Why or why not? Plath had a baby girl, Frieda, before she had her son, Nicholas. If you believe the first voice is the more personal for Plath, why write about the birth of her son rather than of her daughter? She wrote to her mother of the first days at home with Nicholas:

   > I have spent my first whole day up. Things have calmed down considerably, and by next week I think we will be placidly back to schedule . . . the first night the baby came, I couldn't sleep for excitement, and the night after the baby cried all night . . . but now he is settling down to more of a schedule. (*Letters Home* 444)

   How is this excitement at her first days at home with Nicholas similar to the excitement the wife feels at bringing her newborn son home?

2. **Second Voice:** What is the significance of having the woman who is unable to actually bear a child be the woman that is working in a male-dominated culture?

   Do you think there is a connection between the secretary's job and her feelings of being deficient as a woman because of her miscarriage? What might Plath be saying through that connection? Annas sees the secretary's "uncomfortable relationship between self and world" in her speeches and notes that the secretary's words "connect and oppose the world of bureaucracy . . . to her own pregnancy" (87). How do you think the secretary sees that connection to the bureaucracy as responsible for her inability to give birth? How has her engagement in that bureaucracy contributed to that inability? What role does her proximity to the patriarchy play in her miscarriage, in her mind?

3. **Third Voice:** Why make the voice of the woman who gives up her child for adoption a student?

What is significant about the third voice being a college student? Is Plath saying she is not quite a woman yet and therefore not equipped for motherhood? Do you think by the end of the play the student thinks she's missing out, or is she relieved at her decision? What might Plath be saying about women's choices through the voice of the student? Does the student see what would be in store for her and decide she does not want to end up like the other women? Do you think if the student were married she would feel differently about keeping her child? Is marriage the determining factor in her choice, or is it her potential future?

History and Context

Plath's own history plays a role in this play, but that history is firmly rooted in what was happening around her, as well. Plath's own experiences with hospitals and doctors had led her to have some distrust about the institution of medicine; some of that distrust can be seen in this play. Her experiences with childbirth include a miscarriage. In a letter to her mother, she writes of the incident:

> I feel awful to write you now after I must have set you to changing your plans [for a visit to Devon] because I lost the little baby this morning and feel really terrible about it. . . . I looked so forward to sharing a new little baby with you. . . . The doctor said one in four babies miscarry and that most of those have no explanation, so I hope to be in the middle of another pregnancy when you come anyway. (Plath, *Letters Home* 408).

Importantly, however, Plath was also interested in political and social issues, which also surface in this play. As Tracy Brain points out, Plath was aware of environmental issues. She was interested in Rachel Carson's writing about the environment, "expressing concern about the impact of technology on the ecosystem" (Brain 85). Brain also notes, "Plath's environmentalism . . . is concerned with the penetrability of borders of the relationship of any human being to the larger world" and that "Plath's writing insists upon involvement" (85). As you reread the play and consider essay topics, look for Plath's attempts to bring these issues to light.

Sample Topics:

1. **The environment:** How does this play help to demonstrate Plath's concern with the environment?

   How does Plath use this play to make a statement about the environment? She wrote to her mother about her concerns for the future: "I hope the Strontium 90 level doesn't go up too high in milk . . . of course, the Americans have contributed to the poisonous level" (Plath, *Letters Home* 434). Where do you see Plath bringing these issues to readers'/listeners' attention? The First Voice refuses to believe in "those terrible children/Who injure my sleep with their white eyes, their fingerless hands" (Plath 185). This is likely a reference to so-called Thalidomide babies, named after the drug their pregnant mothers took that was blamed for what were termed birth defects. What do you think Plath is saying about these things in this play?

2. **Childbirth for women:** According to this play, how does childbirth, or not being able to give birth, affect a woman's life? Is it considered a woman's biological destiny to have a child?

   What does Plath say about women's role in society through the act of childbirth? Bundtzen sees Plath confirming "the individuality of female response to their bodies. There is no biological destiny to women's emotions" (213). What is more important to society in this play—the physical or the emotional side of the women? Which do you think the women themselves value more? How does the secretary's inability to bear a child make her different from the other two? Why does she blame herself? How does that relate to the student's ability to bear a child but not want to keep it? What do you think Plath is saying about social expectations for women regarding bearing children?

3. **Politics:** Can you identify a political statement in this play? What might Plath be saying about the cultural status of women at this time?

Robin Peel writes of Plath's poetry, especially her later work, "The battle with the 'Other' that is enacted . . . is seen primarily as a gender or personal battle . . . in which the enemy is internalized" (39). How is that battle portrayed in *Three Women*? What or who is the "other" in this play? Peel also argues that Plath wanted to "engage with the wider world, and this dialogue was strongly reexpressed" in some of her later work (40). How do you think Plath is engaging with the wider world in this piece? What concerns about the state of the world do you see her making in this play? How are the statements she makes enhanced by the use of three voices rather than just one?

Form and Genre

This is the only play that Plath wrote, but it still bears many of the trademarks of her poetry, especially that of what is often called her *Ariel* period. Her husband had written a play called *The Wound*, which was performed on the BBC in winter 1962 (Brain 201), so Plath was familiar with the process. She was also confident in *Three Women*, knowing that she was developing a stronger voice and becoming more established in her writing: "There is little question that Plath knew that her late poems, which she characteristically saw as songs or lyrics, were superior to any she had ever written" (Wagner-Martin, *Literary Life* 115). As you read through this play, think about where you see Plath's growing confidence demonstrated in this work.

Sample Topics:

1. **Poem written as a play:** Do you see *Three Women* as a hybrid of poem and play or as a play?

   What is the difference between a standard single-speaker poem and a poem written for multiple voices? How would the messages being shared in this piece be different if it were written as a poem with one speaker/narrator rather than as a play to be read by multiple voices? What is the effect of including more than one voice in a poem? Does that make *Three Women* seem less autobiographical than other of Plath's works? Or does it make it seem more so? Does including more than one voice make the experience being written about seem more individual or more universal? Do you think this play could be read by one person taking on the personas of the three voices, or is it necessary for it to be three separate voices?

2. **Reading out loud:** How do you see Plath's idea of poems as songs or lyrics at work in this play?

   Plath was a big proponent of reading works out loud; especially of her later work she insisted that it was meant to be read that way rather than silently. How is that philosophy especially apparent in this play? What kind of voices (tone, pacing, even volume, etc.) do you imagine in the roles of the three women? Do you picture a celebrity in the role? What is it about the personalities of the voices that helps you come to a decision about these questions? When you read the poem out loud, what do you notice about the different voices? Does Plath's writing style lead you to read the voices with different pacing or different tonality? Does the way any of the voices are written make you feel more or less sympathetic toward one of the three women? How so?

3. **Placement of the speeches:** How is the placement of the individual speeches by the three voices important in this play?

Why do you think Plath chose the arrangement of the speeches by the women in this play? Why not just have them speak all in a row, or take turns, one, two, three? Is one voice privileged over the other two because of the arrangement? Do you think one voice gets more developed than the others? What message do you think Plath is trying to get across by arranging the women's speeches this way? Do you feel like even though the three women are not having an actual conversation with each other, Plath is arranging their words so they are somehow responding to one another's thoughts and fears? What would happen if you dissected the play and rearranged it so the three voices spoke all of their lines in a row rather than breaking it up as Plath has done?

Philosophy and Ideas

Plath's own experiences with pregnancy and childbirth are clear in this poem; she had two children and suffered one late-term miscarriage. Throughout her married life, Plath thought about juggling her roles as a wife, mother, and writer. That struggle can be seen in this play, as well. Before she had children, she considered how they fit into her life; she was happy as a wife and writer/teacher, but she knew that children would eventually be part of her life. In her journals, she writes:

> I am married to a man whom I miraculously love as much as life & I have an excellent job & profession . . . & now will turn to my own profession and devote a year to steady apprenticeship, and to the symbolic counterpart, our children. Sometimes I shiver in a preview of the pain & the terror of childbirth, but it will come & I live through it. (Kukil 336)

This realization and trepidation about childbirth is reflected in this play, as well. Along with that in *Three Women* is an examination of how the act of giving birth changes a woman's life. Plath enjoyed being a mother a great deal, but she also recognized how the responsibilities of motherhood change how a woman goes about her work and life. As you reread the play, consider what Plath is saying about the experiences of women in general, as well, especially when motherhood is introduced into their lives.

Sample Topics:

1. **Ambivalence:** What different feelings about motherhood are presented in this play?

   Bundtzen believes that in this poem, "Plath links her ambivalence—conflicting feelings of women toward their femininity—to her larger view of the world as ruled by a male deity" (217). How do you think the women in this poem feel about their femininity? How is each of the three voices in the play used to reflect this ambivalence? How does the arrangement of the individual "speeches" of the three women help to demonstrate this ambivalence? Would you argue that one or another feeling is stronger than the other? Is there a better term than *ambivalence*, which denotes mixed feelings, that you think is more appropriate to describe the feelings portrayed through the three voices?

2. **Assimilation:** Assimilation is when people from different backgrounds come together; how do you see assimilation being portrayed in this play?

   What does assimilation mean for the women in this play? What would you say is the standard to which the women are assimilating? What is accomplished by their coming together? Which of the three women do you think is most successful in her assimilation? Are there penalties for *not* assimilating? If so, what are they? What are the rewards for assimilation? Do the women have to give up anything to achieve it? If so, do the rewards outweigh the cost? Would you argue that Plath is saying she either assimilated or did not? How is motherhood portrayed as an experience that automatically makes all who experience it part of the same group?

3. **Isolation:** Even though there are three women in the maternity ward that we hear from, the three women never speak to one another. How does that help to illustrate a sense of isolation rather than community?

How are the women in this play isolated? What are they isolated from? Is this isolation of their own choosing, or is it at the hands of someone else, like their culture? How does their isolation make them dependent on others? Plath herself writes of her struggles with these feelings:

> I shall perish if I can write about noone [sic] but myself . . .
> Find always traces of passive dependence: on Ted, on people
> around me. A desire even while I write poems about it, to
> have someone decide my life, tell me what to do, praise me
> for doing it. I know this is absurd. Yet what do I do about it?
> (Kukil 523)

Where do you see this dependence illustrated in the separation of the three women in the play? How does the isolation make the women, as Plath notes of herself, focus on only themselves?

Language, Symbolism, and Imagery

This play offers countless opportunities for a student trying to think of a topic for a paper on language, symbolism, or imagery. As always, one of the best places to start on an essay is to think about what stands out most to you when you read the piece. Is there a particular image or turn of a phrase that you noticed or that you cannot quite forget when you finish reading the play? That can be an excellent place to start.

Another thing to keep in mind is, of course, what you think the writer is trying to accomplish by bringing in these specific images and words. Bundtzen reminds readers of this work that "if we look at the poem's imagery . . . it should remind us of all the poems where Plath is not explicitly speaking in a woman's voice, but simply confronting the 'black, intractable mind' of nature, history, society" (Bundtzen 217). What images do you see in this play that support a point like that? What do you see that makes you disagree with this point? As you decide on a topic, keep in mind what you know or what you think about Plath's entire body of work and how this fits, or does not, with that work.

Sample Topics:

1. **Flatness:** What is the significance of flatness in the play? Who is flat and who is not?

   What is Plath doing when she contrasts the flatness of those around them to the mountainous nature of the pregnant women? Is there something other than not being pregnant that makes people flat? The Third Voice notes of other women around her, "They hug their flatness like a kind of health. / And what if they found themselves surprised, as I did? / They would go mad with it" (Plath 180). Is the flatness she discusses here something to be envied or something to be pitied? How does flatness relate to emptiness in the play—are they the same? As you reread the play, note who exactly is being referred to as flat; what do they have in common? Is it only a lack of pregnancy, or do you think Plath is also saying something about lack of experience, or feeling, or even suffering?

2. **Babies and birth:** What do babies symbolize in this play? What message is Plath conveying through the three different experiences the women in this play have with childbirth?

   In the play, two of the women actually give birth to live babies and one has a miscarriage. What do you think Plath is saying about these women's lives through their experiences with childbirth? What might she be saying about the experiences of women in general? How does having a baby empower a woman in this play? How does it take power away from a woman? What specific message do you think Plath is making in this play by setting it in a maternity ward? What would happen to the message you see being delivered in this poem if it were set somewhere else? Is the same message being communicated in the passages of the play where the women are talking about the experience of childbirth after they leave the ward? How do you see the experience they had with childbirth changing their lives once they leave the maternity ward?

3. **Men:** Why are there no husbands or boyfriends in the maternity ward with the women while they are there?

   Men are strangely absent in the ward in which this play takes
   place, yet they play an important role. What might Plath be
   suggesting by the absence of men in this work? What might
   men symbolize in the context of this play? Bundtzen argues,
   "One of the surprising aspects to the mother's triumph is the
   exclusion of any mention of a father in the waiting, delivery,
   or homecoming. Not so for the secretary and student, who see
   men as powerful victimizers" (214). She also notes "The antagonism between mind and body is between man and woman,
   God and nature. The man thinks and acts, the woman bears
   the consequences. His are the ends, but hers are the means"
   (215). Is Plath saying that even when men are not present, the
   system they have built is still in place? If Bundtzen is right,
   how are men victimizing the secretary (Second Voice) and the
   student (Third Voice)? How might the absence of men in the
   maternity ward actually be a statement Plath is making about
   the presence of men in women's lives?

4. **Religion:** What role does religion play in the lives of the three
   women in the play? What does religion mean to them?

   Although there are not overt references to religion, where
   do you see it being addressed in this work? How is it treated?
   Bundtzen notes, "The secretary and student believe a male
   deity has usurped the woman's body to manifest his ideas, his
   powers . . . The woman who miscarries blames a masculine
   principle for her emptiness" (215). How is the control of this
   deity illustrated throughout the play? What is the significance
   of a deity who takes over a woman's body? Does that same
   deity also take over the women's minds? If not, why not? How
   does the wife (First Voice) feel about this deity? How does she
   talk about her newborn son as if he is a manifestation of this
   deity?

Compare and Contrast

While considering a topic for a compare and contrast essay, it is important to keep in mind that the pieces you are using for the essay are,
indeed, two separate works. In the following suggestions, there are references to authors and works that Plath read or saw and considered
moving or important. Remember that simply because she was inspired
by these authors or admired their work does not mean that she just
copied what they were doing. Look for the complex little things in
Three Women that demonstrate this respect Plath had for other writers and their works rather than thinking of Plath's work as a copy or
imitation of another person's work. If you decide to write your compare
and contrast essay about two works done by Plath, bear in mind that
even if you see some similar themes or ideas in each of the works, she
was expressing those ideas through different genres of writing and at
different times in her life; watch for growth or change from one piece
to another.

Finally, as you consider a compare and contrast essay, again think to
yourself of the purposeful choices made by Plath as she wrote this piece.
How does she use these influences to express her own unique feelings?
Wagner-Martin writes that even though Plath noted inspiration from
Bergman's film *Brink of Life* and Woolf's *The Waves,* "she drew as well on
Dylan Thomas's *Under Milk Wood,* and on the emotions she had known
during her two childbirths, her miscarriage, and her recovery from surgery in the hospital" (*Biography* 199). In other words, beware of breaking
down the work too simply into either homage to another artist or report-
ing of personal experience.

Sample Topics:

1. **To Virginia Woolf's *The Waves:*** How do the three women in
   Plath's play compare to the three women in *The Waves*? Do their
   voices have anything in common?

   It is no secret that Plath greatly admired Woolf, even considering her a role model for women writers. What is the significance
   of the three women in Woolf's novel sharing an experience of
   death (of a friend) and the three women in Plath's play sharing

the experience of life (childbirth)? Where do you see similarities in how the characters from each book deal with the emotions associated with these life events? Woolf includes male characters in her novel; why does Plath leave them out in this play? How do the male characters in Woolf's novel help or hinder the female characters? How do you see Plath addressing that in her play? What issues do you see being dealt with in *The Waves*, published in 1931, that are still important when Plath published this play more than thirty years later?

2. **To "Johnny Panic and the Bible of Dreams":** How do you see medicine being portrayed in these pieces? What is Plath saying through those portrayals?

   "Johnny Panic and the Bible of Dreams" is set in a hospital, as is *Three Women*, and was also inspired by Plath's own experiences in a hospital. What is the biggest difference in the way medicine and hospitals are portrayed in the two stories? What events in Plath's own life do you think contribute to the differences, as well as any similarities, in the portrayals? Is there an overall metaphor or statement you think Plath is making about hospitals and medicine in these works? How does Plath use the setting of a hospital in these works to comment on society as a whole? How does Plath use specific sections of the hospital (the psychiatric ward in "Johnny Panic" and the maternity ward in *Three Women*) to illustrate specific points about medicine and hospitals?

3. **Dylan Thomas's *Under Milk Wood*:** Where do you see the inspiration from Thomas's poem in this play? How might you characterize the use of different voices in each of these works?

   Plath was, by her own admission, quite taken with the poetry of Dylan Thomas. She heard him read *Under Milk Wood* at a reading in 1953 and was struck by the piece (Wagner-Martin, *Biography* 199). Beyond the incorporation of multiple voices, what do you see as a common thread (or common threads) running through these two works? What is accomplished in Thomas's work with the rapid changes through many different voices that is lost in Plath's use of only three voices? What is gained by Plath's use of only three voices? What effect does the use of different voices have in each of these poems? Why use different voices rather than just one?

4. **Ingmar Bergman's film** *Nära Livet,* **or** *Brink of Life:* Why does Plath eliminate men from her retooling of this film?

The Bergman film is likely not an easy one to get, but your school library may be able to help you find it. In the film, which was first shown in 1958, the setting is also a hospital maternity ward. Annas is quick to point out that "though Plath borrowed this basic structure, she made a number of significant changes in characterization and in form" (74). What do you think inspired Plath to build off of this idea of three different women in a maternity ward, going through their own experiences of childbirth? In the film, each of the women has a man in her life; why are there no male characters in this play? How does Plath use the lack of men in her play to say something different than what Bergman was trying to say in his film? What do you see as common messages between the film and the play? Where do you see Plath purposefully veering away from Bergman's story?

Bibliography and Online Resources for *Three Women*

Annas, Pamela. *A Disturbance in Mirrors: The Poetry of Sylvia Plath.* New York: Greenwood P, 1988. Print.

Brain, Tracy. *The Other Sylvia Plath.* Harlow, England: Pearson, 2001. Print.

Bundtzen, Lynda. *Plath's Incarnations: Woman and the Creative Process.* Ann Arbor: U of Michigan P, 1983. Print.

Kukil, Karen V. *The Unabridged Journals of Sylvia Plath.* New York: Anchor Books, 2001.

Peel, Robin. "The Political Education of Sylvia Plath." *The Unraveling Archive: Essays on Sylvia Plath.* Anita Helle, ed. Ann Arbor: U of Michigan P, 2007. 39–62. Print.

Plath, Sylvia. *Three Women: A Poem for Three Voices. The Collected Poems: Sylvia Plath.* Ted Hughes, Ed. New York: Harper Perennial, 2008. Print.

———. *Letters Home.* Ed. Aurelia Plath. New York: Harper and Row, 1975. Print.

Wagner-Martin, Linda. *Sylvia Plath: A Biography.* New York: Simon and Schuster, 1987. Print.

———. *Sylvia Plath: A Literary Life.* Hampshire, England: Macmillan P, 1999. Print.

THE BELL JAR

READING TO WRITE

Plath's *The Bell Jar* is the story of Esther Greenwood, a college student who suffers a mental breakdown, is hospitalized, and ultimately recovers. Because Plath's own life story, including her suicide, is so famous, it is almost impossible *not* to read *The Bell Jar* as a purely autobiographical novel. Although the book is undeniably based on Plath's own experiences, a close reading of the text can help readers understand that there is a lot more to this novel than the story of Sylvia Plath's own mental state. *The Bell Jar* deals with several issues that offer writers many excellent options about which to write.

The Bell Jar was originally published in England in 1963 under the pseudonym Victoria Lucas. From the first, Plath realized the autobiographical nature of the novel might be problematic for her and also for the characters in the book based on people in her life. As Plath herself put it, the book was a "pot-boiler" (Alexander 348). Her mother, Aurelia, was loath to have the book published in the United States after her daughter's death because she feared the damage it might cause and worried about the people "who would be hurt by the book and by the publicity its release would produce" (Alexander 347). It was not until 1971 that the novel was released in the United States, eight years after Plath's death. The fact that the story of Plath's death was already so well known only contributed (and still does) to a reading of Esther Greenwood's story as the story of Plath herself, despite the fact that Plath makes some pointed commentary on social issues in *The Bell Jar* that are often overlooked.

One thing that may help you think about this is to know that Plath herself intended the novel to be something more than just her own story. Plath biographer Linda Wagner-Martin writes, "As she [Plath] reminded herself in her journal, the character of . . . Esther, was to be symbolic: 'Make her a statement of the generation'" (144). Taking this into consideration when reading can help you uncover some of those statements about her generation Plath wanted to make, which can also help you discover essay topics.

Reading for references to events that are going on around Esther is one way to find topics for essays and papers. The first lines of the novel offer readers some historical context for the story of Esther Greenwood and they also provide some foreshadowing:

> It was a queer, sultry summer, the summer they electrocuted the Rosenbergs, and I didn't know what I was doing in New York. I'm stupid about executions. The idea of being electrocuted makes me sick, and that's all there was to read about in the papers—goggle-eyed headlines staring up at me on every street corner and at the fusty, peanut-smelling mouth of every subway. It had nothing to do with me, but I couldn't help wondering what it would be like, being burned alive all along your nerves.
>
> I thought it must be the worst thing in the world.
>
> New York was bad enough. By nine in the morning the fake, country-wet freshness that somehow seeped in overnight evaporated like the tail end of a sweet dream. Mirage-gray at the bottom of their granite canyons, the hot streets wavered in the sun, the car tops sizzled and glittered, and the dry, cindery dust blew into my eyes and down my throat.
>
> I kept hearing about the Rosenbergs over the radio and at the office till I couldn't get them out of my mind. (Plath 1)

Because Esther is eventually hospitalized and receives electroconvulsive therapy (ECT), these opening lines are particularly noteworthy. By considering the fate of Julius and Ethel Rosenberg, who were accused of espionage against the United States during World War II and executed by electrocution, Esther not only foreshadows her own experience with ECT as a sort of execution, but she also suggests a sort of sympathy with the Rosenbergs.

Esther's assertion that thinking about being electrocuted makes her sick and her feeling that electrocution "must be the worst thing in the world" is borne out later in the book when she receives her first ECT treatment and wonders "what terrible thing it was that I had done" (143). Like the Rosenbergs, Esther sees herself as being punished for something. When she notes the execution "had nothing to do with me," her future experiences will show that to not quite be true. What readers can glean from this is also a statement about apathy; when people hear about awful (and, as many experts argue, in the case of the Rosenbergs unjustified) things happening to others, they comfort themselves by thinking it has nothing to do with them.

Another possible topic to consider from this excerpt is the idea of treason. Throughout the novel, Esther struggles to come to terms with what is expected of her—as a young woman, as a writer, as a daughter, as a potential mate—and one of the recurring problems she faces is her disinterest in fulfilling those expectations. At one point, Esther notes that she is not interested in marriage, even saying, "I began to think maybe it was true that when you were married and had children it was like being brainwashed" (Plath 85). Perhaps because of her inability to see typical social conventions like this as favorable, Esther sees herself as a sort of traitor, prompting her fascination with, and perhaps some sympathy with, the Rosenbergs.

These examples are just a few of the things that you can use as you think about a topic for your essay. As you read through the novel and find passages that are particularly interesting to you, think about this notion of Esther making a statement. What kinds of political statements do you see being made? Societal? Look for recurring mentions of specific incidents (such as the Rosenbergs) or conventions (such as marriage) that you think signal a statement Plath is making. You can also think about whether these issues resonate in today's culture, as well. By considering the whole of the book you'll find that although there is much to write about in terms of its reflection of Plath's life and even death, there is also a rich collection of other possible topics that can serve as excellent ideas for papers and essays.

TOPICS AND STRATEGIES

For many writers, one of the most difficult parts of a writing project is getting started. Think of the following ideas and suggestions as ways to help you dig into your writing project and get started rather than as templates or completely formed paper topics. Think of these suggestions as seeds from which you can grow your own ideas for your project. Remember that every reader can find something different in the same text and because you have probably taken part in discussions and other activities related to *The Bell Jar,* you should not discount your own ideas in favor of these. Rather, think of what is put forth here as a way to help you delve into your own reading and ideas about the book. The best papers spring from genuine interest and understanding, so use the topics mentioned here to help you discover those areas where you have the greatest involvement as a reader in the text and that work with your own perceptions about Plath's work.

Themes

Finding themes in a text can be tricky, but close reading can make it easier. To recognize some themes in a piece of literature, think about what you think the writer is trying to say about issues that come up often in the work. Look for clues in everything from character names to dialogue to word choice. In *The Bell Jar* Esther Greenwood wrestles with a lot of issues; those issues make up some of the themes of the book. Some of the themes in this novel are love, sex, marriage, death, mental illness, and social conventions. Another is the idea of doubles, or doppelgangers (a spirit version of a person).

Before you start writing about a theme, though, it is important to figure out what you want to say about it. Often, many readers will see the same theme(s) in a book, so just saying that it is there does not really make for an effective or particularly interesting paper. After you have identified some themes in a book, think about which of them you find most interesting and why you find them interesting. What is it about a certain theme that really stands out to you? Does this theme seem to be emphasized in one character more than others? In one setting? Do you see the theme mainly through characters' thoughts or is it also apparent in their dialogue? Once you have identified some of these points, you are well on your way to deciding on a theme about which to write. Depending on the sort of paper you are writing, you might want to consider whether your purpose for writing is served better by choosing something that might be more obvious (i.e. suicide in *The Bell Jar*) or if you'd be more successful identifying a theme that has not been quite as fully explored as others.

Sample Topics:

1. **Doubles:** Where do you see one person with more than one identity in the novel?

   Because there are so many similarities between her life and that of the author, Esther is often considered Plath's double. Who are Esther's doubles? Why does she create her alter ego, Elly Higginbottom, when she is out with Doreen? Why does Doreen continue to call her Elly, even when they are no longer with Lenny and his friends? Esther sees Elaine, the heroine of the novel she starts when returning home from New York, as another version of herself: "My heroine would be myself, only in disguise. She would be called Elaine. . . . I counted the letters on my fingers. There were six letters in Esther, too. It seemed a lucky thing" (Plath 120). What is significant about when Esther adopts these alter egos?

2. **Marriage:** How does Esther see marriage as different for men than for women? What does she say about women's roles in marriage versus men's roles?

   In one of her journals, Plath writes, "'I am at odds. I dislike being a girl, because as such I must come to realize that I cannot be a man. In other words, I must pour my energies through the direction and force of my mate. My only free act is choosing or refusing that mate'" (qtd. in Wagner-Martin 69–70). How does this quote reflect Esther's views on marriage? Is Esther really against marriage, or is she just against the thought of being "forced" to marry Buddy? Are her mother's and Buddy's mother's efforts to get them together tantamount to an

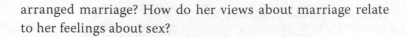

arranged marriage? How do her views about marriage relate to her feelings about sex?

3. **Sex:** Why does Esther see Buddy as a hypocrite and decide she's done with him when she finds out about his affair with the waitress? What is the significance of her saying it happened "on the day we saw the baby born" (Plath 62)?

Reread the section where Buddy tells Esther about his summer affair with the waitress. Esther is angry because she feels like Buddy's been lying to her. What is the significance of her asking Buddy if he's ever had an affair after he's shown her his genitals? Do you think she's jealous of the waitress or just angry at Buddy? Why does she decide she needs to sleep with someone else to make things even? Do you think Esther looks forward to having sex for the first time or just feels like it is something she has got to do?

4. **Betrayal:** Find instances in the novel where Esther feels betrayed by the people around her. How does she express her feelings about these betrayals? Do they seem logical to you, or do you see those feelings as evidence of her upcoming breakdown?

Does Esther feel betrayed by the men in her life, perhaps especially her father and Buddy Willard, more so than by the women in her life? Does Jay Cee betray her by not doing more to help Esther become a professional writer? How does she feel betrayed by her mother? Is Esther betrayed by the system because of her hospitalization and electroconvulsive therapy? Are there bigger statements about society betraying young women who do not fit in being made here?

Characters

Since this novel is so autobiographical in nature, it is hard to separate Plath from Esther Greenwood and to not think about the other characters as actual people in her life. While this is a natural way to think about the characters in *The Bell Jar*, it is important to keep in mind that the book is also a piece of fiction. As Linda Wagner-Martin points out, "*The Bell Jar* is a fiction, and in fiction real people are transformed. Plath's caricatures helped to emphasize the torment of Esther . . . who sees herself as subject to external forces working against her" (190). As you think about what to write, consider how you see the characters—as fictional characters, or as real people. How could that color your treatment of them in a paper? How might any research you do for the project be influenced by your reading?

If you decide on Esther as the focus for your paper, remember that there are a lot of different approaches you can take. While it might seem easiest to write about the main character of a novel, sometimes it can also be overwhelming because there is so much to cover. You might want to consider discussing how the main character deals with a specific event or events or maybe how she interacts with another character. Thinking about how the character is at the beginning of the novel and how she is at the end of the novel can also help you to narrow down what you want to say about her. How might other characters in the novel view her? What do Esther's relationships with some of the other characters in the story say about her? About society in general? About the period in which the book was written?

Characters like Doreen and Joan Gilling, even though they may not be featured throughout the entire book, can make excellent choices for papers. Remembering that every character is placed in the book for a reason, consider what Plath was trying to do by including them in *The Bell Jar*. What role do they play in furthering the story of Esther Greenwood? Does Esther remember their words or actions even when they are not present? How do they reinforce or complicate what Esther hears from other characters? Can they be seen as alter egos for Esther?

Sample Topics:

1. **Esther Greenwood:** Does the fact that Esther is now presumably a wife and mother mean that she's cured? This comes to light in a short section at the beginning of the book, but it is an important part of the story as a whole. What is the effect of Esther's story being told in a sort of flashback like this? What purpose does that serve, especially for readers?

Esther says about the presents from her trip to New York City, "For a long time afterward I hid them away, but later, when I was all right again, I brought them out, and I still have them around the house. I use the lipsticks now and then, and last week I cut the plastic starfish off the sunglasses case for the baby to play with" (Plath 3). What does it mean that she has a child now? What does this say about her recovery? What does it signify that she kept all of those things? That she brought them all out again when she was "all right again"? Do you think Esther thinks she's "all right"? Do you think she ever really thought there was something wrong with her?

2. **Doreen:** What does Doreen signify for Esther? What is it about Doreen that initially draws Esther to her?

Why does Esther ultimately decide of Doreen, "I would watch her and listen to what she said, but deep down I would have nothing at all to do with her. Deep down, I would be loyal to Betsy and her innocent friends. It was Betsy I resembled at heart" (Plath 22). Was it just the fact that Doreen came back to the hotel drunk that made Esther decide this, or was there more? Is Esther afraid of becoming like Doreen? Is she jealous of Doreen's free spirit? What is significant about Doreen not getting sick with ptomaine poisoning while all the other girls were?

3. **Dodo Conway:** What does Dodo Conway signify for Esther? What is the significance of her having more children than anyone else in their neighborhood?

When she sees Dodo walking past her house, Esther says, "Dodo interested me in spite of myself" (116). Is Dodo a frightening figure for Esther or a pathetic one? What is the significance of her being the one to accompany Mrs. Greenwood to the asylum to pick Esther up and bring her home? Does Esther finally find some merit in Dodo, or does Dodo remain a symbol of what Esther does not want in her life? How is Dodo's brood of children related to religion and suburban life for Esther? What does it mean that Dodo's car looks like a hearse?

4. **Buddy Willard:** Does Buddy really love Esther and want to marry her, or is he in his own sort of bell jar?

What effect do you think Buddy's relationship with his mother, which he characterizes as very close, has on his relationship with Esther? How does his bout with tuberculosis and his convalescence at the sanatorium change him? Is it significant that Buddy decides he's falling in love with a nurse at the sanatorium? Why does he want to see Esther to determine whether he still has feelings for her?

History and Context

The Bell Jar was written during the cold war era, a time in the 1950s and 1960s when democratic countries, especially the United States, feared takeover by communist countries such as the USSR and China. As Kathleen Connors points out, Plath "highlighted the Cold War Communist scare in her novel, *The Bell Jar,* which opens with the protagonist's empathetic experience of the Rosenberg executions as spies, and recreates a conversation . . . that reflects some of the facile, anti-Communist rhetoric of the time" (35). The Rosenbergs are mentioned several times in the book, which lends credence to this argument. As you read through *The Bell Jar* preparing for your writing project, look for other references to the cold war and other political issues of the time. You might want to think about what the equivalent of those fears would be today. Thinking of someone Esther's age living in today's world, what would be the news item that would be mentioned most frequently in his or her story?

Another piece of historical context important to *The Bell Jar* is the women's movement. In 1963, Betty Friedan published a book in the United States called *The Feminine Mystique,* which is widely credited with igniting the second wave of feminism in the United States. In her book Friedan claims that women much like Plath's Esther Greenwood, educated young women who wish to pursue something beyond marriage and motherhood, are trapped by societal expectations about women. In this book, Friedan introduces what she calls "the problem that has no name" and argues that women have been taught to "pity the neurotic, unfeminine, unhappy women who wanted to be poets or physicists or presidents. They learned that truly feminine women do not want careers, higher education, [or] political rights" (11). Many critics see *The Bell Jar* as a significant feminist text and Plath as a martyr for the feminist cause.

One more important historical note about the time in which *The Bell Jar* was conceived is the creation of the American suburbs. In post World War II America, the housing development was introduced and Americans began to move from the crowded cities to the more expansive suburbs. In 1947, the first community featuring mass-produced homes, Levittown, New York, was introduced ("A Brief History"). By 1949, home ownership was profoundly changed by this sort of assembly-line approach to building homes, leading to the proliferation of housing developments and a major change to the American way of life. In *The Bell Jar*, Esther talks a lot about being from the suburbs; her trip to New York is a crucial event in her life because it introduces her to life outside of her suburban home and neighborhood, which she finds stifling.

Sample Topics:

1. **The cold war:** Is Esther's experience a personal version of cold war?

   The root of the cold war scare for people in the United States was that communism would take over and democracy, and thus personal freedom, would be lost. Do you see Esther as having the same sorts of fears? As one biographer notes, "Plath carefully sets the story of Esther in the context of a political situation . . . the controversial execution of Julius and Ethel Rosenberg. Esther's personal horror at what she finds in life is set against the horror of their executions" (Wagner-Martin 186). What would take over Esther's life and take away her freedom?

2. **Feminism:** Can *The Bell Jar* be read as a feminist novel?

   Does Esther suffer from the problem that has no name? Read the first chapter of *The Feminine Mystique* and look for passages in *The Bell Jar* that might help you decide whether Esther Greenwood suffers from "the problem that has no name." What concerns does Esther Greenwood have about her life, and especially her writing, if she marries? Note the women in the novel who are married and those who are not. What effects do those women have on Esther? Who are the women that Esther really admires? Do they uphold feminist ideals? How or how not?

3. **The city versus the suburbs:** How does Esther's experience in New York City change her outlook on her future? How is that outlook affected when she returns home to her suburban neighborhood?

When Esther finds out that she has not been accepted for the summer writing course, she is devastated. Is her upset solely because she cannot attend the class, or is it also because she will be "sentenced" to the suburbs for the summer? Think of the women Esther encounters in the city versus those she encounters back at home. How are those women symbolic of what Esther sees as her choices? Discuss how the setting where Esther is situated affects her state of mind. Why does Esther break down when she is asked to pose for a photo demonstrating her career plans? Is there an argument that she knows her time in the city is coming to a close and she's worried about what her future holds when she returns home?

Philosophy and Ideas

Deciding what sorts of philosophies are put forth in a text can be difficult. One way to determine what philosophy an author might be putting forth in a book or poem is to look for what you think the writer is saying about something big. Unlike some of the other things discussed here, like themes and imagery, philosophy is a bit less specific but deals with major issues; thinking of philosophy as the sum of all of these might help. When you are done reading a text, think about what you take away from it, and that might also help you determine the main ideas and philosophy of the text.

Another way to think about the philosophy embodied in a text is to think about what the text says about life in general or what the author says in the piece that applies outside of the text. For instance, despite the fact that *The Bell Jar* is nearly a half century old, it still has a lot to say to contemporary readers. As one writer says of the novel, "The big questions: how to sort out your life, how to work out what you want, how to deal with . . . sex, how to be true to yourself and how to figure out what that means—those things are the same today" (McCullough xvi). As you prepare to write about *The Bell Jar,* consider how relevant the issues Esther faces are in the lives of young people today.

Sample Topics:

1. **Control:** Who does Esther think is in control of her life? Is she correct, or is her perception about control part of what leads to her breakdown?

   Throughout her story, Esther seems to be trying to decide what to do with herself. Is she experiencing the normal pangs of independence for someone her age? Is her life actually being determined by forces beyond her control? How much responsibility does Esther take for her actions and for what happens to her? Does she actually have more control over her own fate than she realizes?

2. **Power:** What kinds of power are exhibited in the novel? Who has that power?

   Do the people who have power have anything in common? Does Esther gain power by resisting adherence to societal norms for women her age, or does she lose power? Read the section where Esther takes the sleeping pills and hides herself under the house. By attempting to commit suicide, is Esther actually trying to exert power, or is she illustrating her powerlessness to function in the world around her?

3. **Reality:** How does the reality of Plath's life play out in *The Bell Jar*? Does Esther seem like a reliable narrator for a story that is both hers and Plath's?

One way to get a new perspective on Esther as narrator of Plath's life is to read about Plath's life, like a biography of Sylvia Plath (there are two listed in the bibliography for this chapter), or the collection of Sylvia's letters to her mother, titled *Letters Home,* or some of Plath's journals that are available in several books. Do you see specific events mentioned in each that are treated either much alike or very differently?

Form and Genre

The Bell Jar is categorized as fiction, although there is little argument that it is a largely autobiographical piece. Because of the autobiographical nature of the book, the first-person-narrative form offers an especially immediate point of view. One way to think about the form of a novel is to examine the structure of it. Is the story told chronologically or out of order? In this case, the story is actually a flashback, told by Esther after she's survived her breakdown and presumably recovered. Throughout the novel there are hints of what is to come, but it is not until she attempts to kill herself that the depth of Esther's problems becomes clear. Thinking of how the lead-up to her breakdown is presented to readers, especially by an author who underwent the events about which she's writing, can help you to consider some of the choices the author made and how the novel's effect would be changed if the story were told differently.

Sample Topics:

1. **Coming of age:** How does *The Bell Jar* differ from more traditional coming of age stories? How does it adhere to the conventions of the style?

   Frances McCullough notes that the novel "quickly established itself as a female rite-of-passage novel" when it was published in the United States (xiv). What are the rites that Esther undergoes? What is the major event that sparks the important change in Esther? It might be easy to assume it is the electroconvulsive therapy, but is there an argument for another event as the climax and turning point? What is the lesson that Esther learns that she can take away from this experience?

2. **Bildungsroman:** This is a style of story that details the psychological growth of the main character. How does *The Bell Jar* fit this genre of story?

This style of story emphasizes the difficult transition of the protagonist, especially as he or she faces expectations of society, into adulthood. How is this different than a coming of age story? Which seems more appropriate to describe Esther's story? What would you identify as the important events along the way that signal Esther's growth? Is the fact that Esther is telling her story evidence of her psychological growth? Detail the expectations of 1950s American society that served as the obstacles Esther had to overcome. Did she overcome any of them? Was it her treatment at the asylum that allowed her to do so?

3. **Poet as novelist:** How is Plath's penchant for writing poetry evident in this novel?

The Bell Jar is Plath's only novel; her other published work is mostly poetry. As Jo Gill points out, "For some early critics . . . *The Bell Jar* was best thought of as 'a poet's notebook' or as 'a poet's novel, a casebook almost in stanzas' (73). Does this criticism seem valid to you? As you read through the novel, note places where there are references to poetry. Is poetry privileged over other forms of writing by Esther? Choose a passage and look at turns of phrase or images that seem suited to poetry. Study one of Plath's poems, such as "Daddy," and look for similar imagery and word choice. What connections do you see between the novel and those poems? Look at which came out first and discuss how you see one influencing the other.

4. **Epistolary features:** How does the incorporation of newspaper headlines and clippings and Esther's own writing influence the telling of Esther's story?

The novel begins with Esther's consideration of the newspaper headlines about the execution of the Rosenbergs. While she is in the asylum, Joan reveals the newspaper clippings she has saved about Esther's suicide attempt. What does this documentation of death and attempts to die mean in this story? How is Esther affected when she sees the clippings Joan has saved? What might Plath be saying about the public's fascination with death and dying? What might she be saying about fame and what people will do to achieve it? How does the story Esther is writing when she is home for the summer reflect her desire to become a famous writer? How do you think Plath would feel about her own journals being published, unabridged, after her death? Consider the implications of reading Plath's works while also being able to read her own words about some of those works.

Language, Symbols, and Imagery

There are myriad symbols and images in *The Bell Jar*. The image of the bell jar itself is obviously crucial to the story, but there are other recurring images that offer many opportunities for analysis. Birth and death, in many different forms, are common images in the book. When Esther joins Buddy for his rounds at medical school, she is unmoved by the sight of cadavers, including "big glass bottles full of babies that had died before they were born" (63). This odd juxtaposition of birth and death can also be read as symbolic of Esther's own ambivalence toward life and death. Her lack of feeling is another recurring issue in the novel; she often realizes that she should be feeling something but is not feeling anything or is not feeling what she knows is the "right" emotion. Because life and death are such emotional events in a person's life, Esther's inability to experience those emotions further illustrates her problematic mental state.

Once you find an image or a symbol or a particular passage that resonates with you, reread the novel to find all the mentions of it in the book. Note the places they appear; can you decipher a particular pattern to those appearances? Are the images or phrases paired with certain events or characters? How are they used to emphasize a theme or an idea in the novel as a whole? Answering some of these questions can help you to put together a solid foundation for a writing project.

Sample Topics:

1. **The bell jar:** Examine the places in the book where Esther talks about being in the bell jar. How does the image of the bell jar, trapping her and distorting what she sees outside of the bell jar, seem appropriate to Esther's descriptions of her life and her feelings?

   A bell jar captures what is underneath it, but it also puts it on display. How does this relate to Esther? She notes that it would not matter where she was, she would always "be sitting under the same glass bell jar, stewing in my own sour air" (185). Does the mention of her "own sour air" indicate a belief that she is part of the problem the bell jar presents for her? Esther also says she can never be sure that the bell jar will not descend on her again; does this seem like a valid concern?

2. **Birth and babies:** What is the significance of babies in *The Bell Jar*? When Esther watches Mrs. Tomolillo give birth to her son, she thinks, "the most important thing to me was actually seeing the baby come out of you yourself and making sure it was yours" (67). What in Esther's experience makes you think she'd be concerned about this rather than other aspects of giving birth?

   Why does Esther pair her realization that Buddy is a hypocrite with the statement, "I found out on the day we saw the baby born" (62)? After her ECT, Esther says that she is reborn. How does this change the tone of the birth references in the novel? When she's watching Dodo Conway walk past her house with all of her kids, Esther states, "Children made me sick" (117). Is the past tense indicative that this is no longer the case? What does it mean that at the beginning of the book Esther refers to her child as "the baby" instead of by name? What is symbolized by her cutting apart the treasures from her trip to New York City for her baby?

3. **Headlines and newspapers:** What role do headlines play in making statements about the major events in the novel?

The story of the Rosenbergs is one of the first to be told via headlines, as outlined at the beginning of this chapter. The other notable mentions of headlines are related to Esther's suicide attempt. What is the connection between the two events? When Esther is in the asylum, Joan Gilling presents her with a cache of clippings she saved from the newspaper reports of Esther's disappearance when she attempted to kill herself. Why Joan? What does it mean that she saved them? Is she jealous of Esther because of Buddy Willard? Does Joan actually feel camaraderie with Esther (after showing her the collection of clippings, she tells Esther about her own suicide attempt)? What does it mean that it is one of the photos Dodo Conway took of Esther and her mother and brother that is featured in the newspaper? Does the fact that Esther's personal drama played out in the headlines connect to the idea of the bell jar being something that traps her yet puts her on display?

4. **The fig tree:** Look at the first time the fig tree is introduced. Is it significant that she reads it as she's recovering from ptomaine poisoning? Do you think Esther understands the full significance of the fig tree image the first time she reads the story?

Many writers have discussed the fig tree: "A central image of the book, the fig tree bearing ripe figs, depicts the female dilemma of the 1950s. No woman can have it all, but choosing is also difficult" (Wagner-Martin 185). Does this explanation of the fig tree image fit with Esther's own experiences? Later on in the novel, she says, "I saw my life branching out before me like the green fig tree from the story" but later says, "I saw myself sitting in the crotch of this fig tree, starving to death, just because I couldn't make up my mind which of the figs I would choose . . . and, as I sat there, unable to decide, the figs began to wrinkle and go black, and, one by one, they plopped to the ground at my feet" (Plath 77). Is it significant that she thinks this as she thinks about her date with Constantin? Is the mention of the dead figs another case of foreshadowing of what's to come for Esther?

Compare and Contrast Essays

Compare and contrast essays are a useful way to analyze two elements of a piece of literature thoroughly. They can also help to understand and explain different points of view. One thing to be careful of when writing a compare and contrast essay is oversimplifying the comparisons. You do not want your essay to seem like a tennis game that just goes back and forth between the elements you are analyzing; think of creating a thesis statement and an organizational structure for your paper that allows you to dig into some specific aspects of each of the things you are looking at rather than running through a list of similarities and dissimilarities.

Sample Topics:

1. *The Bell Jar* **and Virginia Woolf's** *Mrs. Dalloway:* Compare and contrast Esther Greenwood and Clarissa Dalloway.

   Kathleen Connors notes that "Many critics have written of Sylvia Plath's literary debt to Virginia Woolf" (118). One Plath biographer claims "Plath used *Mrs. Dalloway* . . . as a template for *The Bell Jar*" (Connors 119). Read *Mrs. Dalloway* and compare Clarissa Dalloway to Esther Greenwood. What sorts of things do they have in common? Both are middle-class or upper-middle-class women; do they deal with different issues or are they actually much the same? Like Esther Greenwood, Clarissa Dalloway is dealing with issues of war (World War I had just ended) and pondering marriage as well as her future. Do these sound like the same sorts of thing Esther Greenwood was pondering? How might you use historical context from each of the novels (1925 for *Mrs. Dalloway* and 1961/1973 for *The Bell Jar*) to come to some conclusions about the similarities and dissimilarities of their situations?

2. *The Bell Jar* **and J. D. Salinger's** *The Catcher in the Rye:* Compare and contrast the story of Esther Greenwood to that of Holden Caulfield.

   Many critics say that *The Bell Jar* bears a strong resemblance to *The Catcher in the Rye* and that Esther Greenwood is in

many ways a female version of Holden Caulfield. How does the
time both spend in New York City help them discover themselves? How do their experiences in mental health institutions
differ? Are both of them considered mentally ill because of
their failure to fit into cultural expectations for them? Why is
Holden so upset and unnerved by what he sees as Mr. Anto-
lini's sexual advances, while Esther is basically unmoved by
Joan's? What does that say about the ways in which each of the
narrators is presented? About gender roles?

3. **Doreen and Betsy:** Compare and contrast Doreen and Betsy,
especially regarding their demeanor during the New York City
trip as described by Esther.

Why is Esther drawn to each of these girls, yet cannot seem to
quite attach herself to either? She eschews Betsy and the other
girls to go out with Doreen, yet after she goes out with Doreen,
she says she is like Betsy at heart. What is it about each of the
girls that both draws Esther in and repulses her? How do the
characteristics, including the physical appearance, of each girl
reflect, or even complicate, Esther's views of herself?

4. *The Bell Jar*'s **reception in England in 1963 and the United
States in 1971:** *The Bell Jar* was published under two different
names in two different countries at two different times. What
sorts of changes occurred in those eight years that would influence the reception of the novel?

How were things different for women? Compare what was
going on in England in 1963 and what was happening in the
United States in 1971. Was the novel considered a feminist
text when it first came out in England? What made feminists
and feminist critics see it as a feminist statement when it was
released in the United States? How did Plath's suicide affect
the reception of her book? Do you think that *The Bell Jar* would
have been as popular if Plath had not committed suicide? Why
or why not? When it was released in England, it got some good

reviews, but many were lukewarm. Why would her death and the resulting realization of the autobiographical nature of the book make it so much more popular when it was rereleased?

Bibliography and Online Resources for *The Bell Jar*

Alexander, Paul. *Rough Magic: A Biography of Sylvia Plath*. New York: DeCapo, 1999. Print.

"A Brief History of Levittown." *Levittownhistoricalsociety.org*. Levittown Historical Society. n.d. Web. 20 Dec. 2009.

Connors, Kathleen. "Living Color: The Interactive Arts of Sylvia Plath." *Eye Rhymes: Sylvia Plath's Art of the Visual*. Kathleen Connors and Sally Bayley, Eds. Oxford: Oxford U P, 2007. Print.

Friedan, Betty. *The Feminine Mystique*. New York: Dell, 1963.

Gill, Jo. *The Oxford Introduction to Sylvia Plath*. Cambridge: Cambridge U P, 2008. Print.

McCullough, Frances. Foreword. ix–xvii. 1996. Plath, Sylvia. *The Bell Jar*. New York: Harper Collins, 1971. Print.

Plath, Sylvia. *The Bell Jar*. New York: Harper Collins, 1971. Print.

Wagner-Martin, Linda. *Sylvia Plath: A Biography*. New York: Simon and Schuster, 1987. Print.